Journey to a
Brave New World

Journey to a Brave New World

The Startling Evidence That Humanity Is Being Manipulated Towards a Very Grim Future—but We Can Change Direction

David Watts

iUniverse, Inc.
Bloomington

JOURNEY TO A BRAVE NEW WORLD
THE STARTLING EVIDENCE THAT HUMANITY IS BEING MANIPULATED TOWARDS A VERY GRIM FUTURE—BUT WE CAN CHANGE DIRECTION

iUniverse books may be ordered through booksellers or by contacting:

iUniverse
1663 Liberty Drive
Bloomington, IN 47403
www.iuniverse.com
1-800-Authors (1-800-288-4677)

ISBN: 978-1-4759-7482-9 (sc)
ISBN: 978-1-4759-7484-3 (hc)
ISBN: 978-1-4759-7483-6 (ebk)

Library of Congress Control Number: 2013902506

Printed in the United States of America

iUniverse rev. date: 03/23/2013

If you have been sent this book as a gift it's because the sender cares for you and your family. They have sent it because humanity is in danger and the people must awaken to the realities of our world. Please respect them by reading it—what you do afterwards is up to you.

ACKNOWLEDGEMENTS

Special thanks goes to Robert Roselli for editing suggestions and allowing me to have a regular voice on his radio show.

To Alex Jones of Infowars.com for providing the daily inspiration and courage to try and make a difference.

To Mo for triggering my awakening.

And to my wife and family who have been so supportive during my awakening process and throughout.

"Our life together is so precious together.
We have grown, we have grown"

—John Lennon, (Just Like) Starting Over

TABLE OF CONTENTS

INTRODUCTION

For as long as I can remember I always felt that something wasn't quite right with the World and many of the events that had taken place, but it wasn't until the late Fall of 2006 that the painful truth of one such event triggered me to seek more answers and my awakening started it's long and sometimes difficult, but ultimately rewarding journey.

In November 2006 around the forty third anniversary of the assassination of John F. Kennedy, I flew from my home on the East Coast to Orange County, California to assist my best friend of many years with closing down his failing business. It wasn't long after being picked up from the airport before we started talking of the JFK conspiracy and several other similar events for which we both heartily agreed on, but then my friend brought forth the suggestion that another, more recent event (for which I will cover in this book) was NOT what it seemed. For several hours we argued and it had crossed my mind to get back to airport as quickly as possible and head back home for I really didn't want to hear what he had to say, but I decided that he deserved some respect and at that I should least take a look at the evidence he claimed to have.

As I looked through the claims and evidence, I was taken aback and overwhelmed with emotions of which chief among them was anger. I was not at all happy about what I was seeing and hearing, but I was also not able to logically counter any of the evidence. My only responses were "how can that be?" and "why?". So upon returning home a few days later I set out to prove that what was being claimed was false. I spent hundreds of hours researching the official claims and watching the archived news videos and reading the mainstream media accounts and compared it the new information I had, but more importantly I tried to set my emotions aside and research it from a logical perspective and after several weeks I came to the conclusion and realization that the facts of this event were definitely not what the mainstream media and all other so called "experts" were pushing. We had indeed been lied to. But the answer to why, was something I couldn't work out at that time.

I knew though that I couldn't just leave it at that, I felt a strong need to dig deeper and to answer that essential question of "why"? At the same time I attempted to force this information on others—not the best strategy in most cases. I lost many good friends with this approach.

I spent five years working to get my Engineering Degree, but I've spent over six years and several thousand hours of solid research which has taken me down hundreds of 'rabbit holes' and uncovered some startling truths, much of which is in plain sight of all us. We just need the triggers and a deprogramming process to see it. Once you've gone through this deprogramming process, for those that are able to, you will also see that yes, the Emperor really is naked.

I also have to admit there are some rabbit holes that I know exist because I've taken a peak, but I have deliberately not dug too deep—at least at the moment. However, in my research I have also uncovered some truly wonderful truths which will be incorporated into the subject of a future book and I have encountered some truly wonderful new friends.

This book is written for those that like me, six years ago, can feel that something is not right with the world but can't quite put the pieces together. I ask that if you find something in this book that sounds way too crazy, please put the book down, research what I have said and once my points have been proven, continue reading. Truth is often stranger than fiction.

I hope this book helps you to embark on a journey of truth that you will find equally enlightening and help you to change your life in a positive way. Have no fear, just LOVE!

Important note

Due to U.S. Copyright laws there are certain restrictions on the amount of material or quotes that can be used, therefore I will provide as much as I can, whilst staying within the confines of the law, but will also provide the internet search terms that will direct you to the materials or quotes.

CHAPTER 1

Its a mad, mad, mad, mad World

There can be no denying that we are living in a seemingly crazy world, a world upside down and back to front. It seems like every day the mainstream news media is bombarding us with news stories that, if looked at logically just doesn't make sense, but for most people they have now turned off any logical thoughts of their own and are just accepting the facts that are presented to them by the experts in suits or skirts on our television screens, just as Zbigniew Brzezinski implied in his book 'Between Two Ages' and just as Lord Bertrand Russell said in his 1931 book, 'The Scientific Outlook',

"The society of experts will control propaganda and education".

Has the vast majority of our supposedly well educated population really lost the ability to discern when something is not quite right with the news and information they are being presented with? Have they been *programmed* to the point of no return? Let's take a look at a few news headlines from the last few months and years. If you, the reader, think all is well . . . there is nothing to see here . . . Then please move on, this book is not for you.

1

The Business Insider, September 13th 2012,—"The Fed Just Announced Unlimited QE"

This means that the Private, yes Private run for profit Central Bank of the United States called the Federal Reserve can now create as much money as it likes and loan it to our Government at interest. In early September of 2012 the official U.S. National Debt climbed above $16 Trillion, or to put it another way $140,000 of debt per taxpayer. Unlimited *Quantitative Easing* will increase the money supply leading to hyperinflation just as it did in the Weimar Republic during the 1920's and will leave the U.S. taxpayers with a debt that can never be paid off. We will explore more about the banking system in the next chapter.

The Daily Mail (UK), November 27th 2012—"A human Will Always Decide When a Robot Kills You: Pentagon's reassurance over fears of machine apocalypse."

In this article it explains that the Department of Defense issued a new policy directive saying that any semi-autonomous weapons systems will be designed so they need human authorization to open fire. The article details concerns from Human Rights Watch who are calling for a ban on *killer robots*.

We've already seen what semi-autonomous weapons systems can do with humans at the trigger. Just perform an internet search on the term 'Drone kills civilian' and you'll found literally millions of articles detailing how a drone was used in an attempt to kill a 'target', but that civilians were accidently killed or caught in the line of fire. So the Pentagon's re-assurance that some young man, or woman, who has spent most of their young life trained on XBOX and PLAYSTATION to shoot and kill anything on-site is hardly comforting. It might also concern you to know that in an unclassified document issued in July 2011 by Robotics System Joint Project Office titled 'Unmanned Ground Systems Roadmap', says under the heading 'Future Trends'—

> "As UGV missions continue to expand, the requirements placed on UGV's will constantly rise. There is an ongoing push to increase UGV autonomy, with a current goal of 'supervised autonomy', but with an ultimate goal of full autonomy."

So who is telling us the truth? The Pentagon via our mainstream media is telling us they will never allow fully autonomous systems to kill, yet military documents say they will.

Examiner and Daily Mail, October 1st 2012—"Former Priest hired by TSA to pat down passengers, three months after church kicked him out for 'molesting young girls'".

This news headline took 10 years to surface. Thomas Harkin was 'released' from the Diocese of Camden in 2002 after a second allegation of molesting a young girl. He was hired by the TSA three months later.

The TSA attempted to defend themselves by stating:

> "in the wake of the September 11th 2001 terrorist attacks there was an urgent need for agents and that meant that staff were being hired without being put under sufficient scrutiny . . . . 50,000 workers were employed at the same time as Harkins, an unnamed TSA official said, many of whom went through without checks."

The article goes on to state that the church did notify the TSA in writing in 2003, but that no action was taken.

Apart from the fact that no action was taken despite this knowledge, what I find most disturbing is that these TSA agents were employed without background checks and yet they are supposed to be part of the front line in the so called war against terror. In fact on the TSA's own website http://www.tsa.gov/careers it states "Security is the TSA's highest priority". What could be the repercussions if they employed a suspected terrorist rather than a pervert? I guess in a way it's a good job that these agents don't perform at the same careless levels as their bosses do. You have to admit they are very thorough, especially if you fit into their 'perversion preference' or if they just don't like the look of you. Just take a look at these two headlines:

Dallas news channel (PIX 11), April 28, 2011—"Former Miss USA says TSA agent 'touched my vagina'".

And from

Daily Mail, December 2nd 2012—"TSA agent pulls down dress to expose the breasts of 17-year-old niece of Congressman during airport pat-down as he demands federal investigation"

Again, search on the Internet for 'TSA agent accused' and you'll find millions about articles of TSA agents touching, groping, molesting or stealing from passengers. But perhaps I'm in the minority in thinking that something is wrong here. You certainly have to wonder when results in a recent Harris poll showed that 35% of Americans said they would wear 'electric shock bracelet' in order to fly.

Let's take a look at a headline from October 9th 2009.

"Obama Wins Nobel Peace Prize"

According to many news outlets including the Huffington Post, October, 9, 2009

> "The announcement drew gasps of surprise and cries of too much, too soon. Yet President Barack Obama won the Nobel Peace Prize on Friday because the judges found his promise of disarmament and diplomacy too good to ignore."

So our President is awarded the Nobel Peace Prize on a 'promise'. Well I promise to bring world peace as soon as I'm elected—is that enough to get me nominated this year? Still, President Obama has to be congratulated because other great world leaders like Benito Mussolini (1935), Adolf Hitler (1939) and Joseph Stalin (1945 and 1948) were nominated but just missed out on winning it themselves. Just as well because they went on to being responsible for the deaths of over 30 million people—how embarrassing would that have been for the Nobel Peace Prize Panel? Although it makes you wonder how many millions will die under Obama's rule? This is a serious question, especially when in May 2012 the NY Times reports that:

"Secret 'Kill List' proves a test of Obama's Principles and Will"

The article explains that—

> "This was the enemy, served up in the latest chart from the intelligence agencies:...The mug shots and brief biographies resembled a high school yearbook layout. Several were Americans...including a girl who looked even younger than her 17 years."

Now when I took my civics test to become an American citizen I don't recall anything about the Executive Branch of Government having the Right to kill a U.S. Citizen without a proper trial. Interestingly we find another link with Obama to Hitler and Stalin since they both had 'Kill Lists' too. Stalin's kill list was rather long and included about 20 million Ukrainians, whereas Hitler's Kill list included several million Jews and Charlie Chaplin—because he thought he was Jewish. (Source: Mail Online: February 27, 2008)

Everyone should have the right to plead their case to a jury of their peers. Secret 'Kill Lists' are not indicative of a truly free nation.

You don't have to be a Christian to know that something is very wrong when headlines such as:

USA Today, November 25th 2012—"Palm Scanner get thumbs up is schools, hospitals"

The article explains that:

> "At schools in Pinellas County, Fla., students aren't paying for lunch with cash or a card, but with a wave of their hand over a palm scanner."

Mark of the Beast do I hear you cry? Whether you are religious or not this should give you a major cause for concern. When Aaron Russo, a film producer and director blew the whistle on a meeting he had with Nick Rockefeller where he was being offered to join 'them', he explained that Rockefeller had told him that 'their' ultimate goal is to implant everyone with an RFID chip.(Source: video interview with Alex Jones) Slowly we are being trained to take what seems to be small and inconsequential steps. You'll hear of hospital patients accepting a tiny 'insert' to help doctors identify patients and the medications they are taking. You will also start hearing more about a 'cashless society' and instead of Dollars we will be able to purchase goods and service using a system of 'Credits'. Step by step by step and before you know it people will look back and ask "how on earth did we get here?" I will cover this in more details further in this book.

Another headline that may not surprise you but should still cause concern is:

Hattiesburg America.com, November 26th 2012—"Black Friday Gun Sale Checks Hit Record"

> 'Washington for the second consecutive year, prospective gun buyers joined Black Friday shoppers in record numbers as firearms dealers swamped FBI with required buyer background check requests'

Barack Obama can confidently claim that he has done more for the firearms industry than any other President. The second Amendment to our Constitution and the Bill of Rights were specifically written to counter the threat of a tyrannical government taking over. And it's not just the citizens getting ready either. There are hundreds of articles detailing unusually large purchases, or contracts to purchase, made by the Department of Homeland Security (DHS). Research by 'INFOWARS.COM' into known contracts between DHS and firearms manufactures showed that between November 2011 and November 2012 various departments within DHS and including Social Security Administration and NOAA contracted for at least 1.6 Billion rounds of ammo. That's enough to put more than four bullets into every U.S. citizen, regardless of age. The ammo is not just regular target shooting ammo either. In one Government solicitation detailed on the FedBizOpps.gov website the DHS required 176,000 rounds of .308 which is a deadly bullet used in sniper rifles. The largest percentage of total ammunition purchased by the DHS are for Hollow Points rounds. Evidence suggest that Hollow Points are banned for use in the regular army during times of conflict because of the devastating damage they do to the victim. Hollow Points are also much more expensive compared to normal practice rounds, so the question is: Why does the DHS need such a quantity of highly lethal ammo and who are they expecting to kill?

For the last couple of decades we have been inundated with claims of 'Global Warming' and 'Climate Change'. We are given images of Polar Bears clinging to small pieces of ice. We have seen advertisements on our Televisions showing children's heads being blown up because they didn't go along with the global warming story. Okay, now that's it, I hear you say. You don't believe that I bet. Well put the book down, and do an internet search using "global warming advert blowing up"—no pressure . . .

Man Made Global Warming is a HOAX! How do I know this? Well apart from researching real science, not junk science paid for by the Central Bankers, you can also read a document by a United Nation 'Think Tank' called the Club of Rome titled "The First Global Revolution". In that document it reads:

"In searching for a new enemy to unite us, we came up with the idea that pollution, the threat of global warming, water *shortages, famine and the like would fit the bill . . . All these dangers are caused by human intervention and it is only through changed attitudes and behaviour that they can be overcome. The real enemy, then, is humanity itself."*

I also encourage you to research the cycles of warming and cooling that the earth naturally goes through. (Source: longrangeweather.com) Take for example Britain around 1200 A.D. where living structures were built without an inside fireplace. This was because the earth was going through a 'warm cycle' and therefore they did not need it. However from the late 1600's to the mid 1800's the River Thames regularly froze during the winter, something you don't see now.

Surprisingly the UK's Daily Mail online news service published an article on January 29, 2012 with the following title:

"Forget Global Warming—it's Cycle 25 we need to worry about (and if NASA scientists are right the Thames will be freezing over again)—Met Office releases new figures which show no warming in 15 years."

The article explains that "Based on readings from more than 30,000 measuring stations, the data was issued last week without fanfare by the Met Office and the University of East Anglia Climatic Research Unit. It confirms that the rising trend in world temperatures ended in 1997."

Finally the last argument that I shall deal with on this matter is based on a **National Geographic article from February 2007 titled "Mars Melt Hints at Solar, Not Human Cause For Warming, Scientists Say"**

Scientists have discovered that at the same time earth appears to warming so too are other planets in our Solar System including Mars. Just how many cars and CFC filled refrigerators do they have on Mars? Perhaps that big bright yellow circle that appears in the sky everyday just might have something to do with it.

Now we're going to take a look at another article and document that will have you reaching for your computer (and quite possibly the toilet bowl as it certainly made me feel sick when I first read it) because I'm sure you will find this hard to believe too.

In March 2012 Alberto Giubilini and Francesca Minerva co-authored a paper that was published in the Medical Ethics Journal, a subset of the British Medical Journal and British Medical Association titled:

"After-Birth Abortion: Why should the baby live?

The authors of this paper argue that newborns are still only "potential persons" and no different to a fetus and therefore since we legally allow for fetuses to be aborted it should be no different for the newborn to be aborted "including cases where the newborn is not disabled".

The paper describes how they prefer to call the procedure After Birth Abortion rather than infanticide to emphasize that the moral status of the individual killed is comparable with that of a fetus.

They state:

> "If the death of a newborn is not wrongful to her on the grounds that she cannot have formed any aim that she is prevented from accomplishing, then it should also be permissible to practice an after-birth abortion on a healthy newborn too, given that she has not formed any aim yet."

The paper concludes by stating that they do not suggest any age thresholds as it depends on the neurological development of the newborn and that neurologist and psychologists would be best able to determine at what age the newborn has aims and therefore would not meet the criteria.

The Internet search term (if you can stomach reading the paper) is:
AFTER BIRTH ABORTION PDF

For me I can only describe this as one of the most disgusting documents I've had the displeasure of reading. I find their argument that because a baby, (with no stated age limits), does not have any 'aims' in life makes it perfectly okay to murder that baby, totally and absolutely abhorrent.

I'm sure many readers will argue that this could never be passed into law or practiced in the real world—a good argument, or so you'd think, but let's now look at a practice that was carried out 'legally' at least 40,000 times in the U.S. from 1995 to 2003 called Partial Birth Abortion. In September 1992 Martin Haskell presented a technique at the National Abortion Federation Seminar called 'Partial Birth Abortion'. It describes how the cervix is dilated (using drugs) such that the abortionist (I really struggle here to call the people that would do this 'Doctors') is able to pull the baby out by the legs leaving just its head inside. The abortionist then takes a special pair of scissors and while keeping the baby still inserts the sharp scissors into the back of the baby's skull piercing the brain. They then open up the scissors to make sure they finish the job. They clean up by suctioning the brain out.

The Partial Birth Abortion Act was passed in the U.S. House in September 1995 and passed in the U.S. Senate in December 1995, just three years after it was suggested.

Now let's not forget a quote from the Founder of Planned Parenthood, Margaret Sanger, taken from her book published in 1920 titled 'Women and the new race' chapter five, 'The wickedness of creating large families'—"The most merciful thing that a large family does to one of its infant members is to kill it".

Planned Parenthood proudly announced that for their fiscal year 2011-2012 they aborted 333,964 babies, effective to one baby killed every 94 seconds.

The chairwoman of Planned Parenthood in an introductory letter to their Annual Report said.

> "We are so proud of the year's many successes, and deeply grateful for all the partners, sponsors, volunteers, staff and friends who helped make them possible,"

Today we have many other examples of similar sentiment from people like Bill Gates who while attending the Aspen Idea Festival in Aspen Colorado in the summer of 2010, discussed the use of "death panels" and argued the case for "killing Granny", by explaining that he felt it was money well saved to euthanize someone who may only have a few months to live as that money could help fund more teachers. We will be detailing more *wonderful and insightful* thoughts from Bill Gates later in this book.

To conclude this subject let's now look at a news article from the:

Daily Mail, November 28th 2012—"Now Sick Babies go on death plan pathway: Doctor's haunting testimony reveals how children are put on end of life plan"

The article details how the practice of withdrawing food and fluid by tube was being used on young patients, also how a Doctor admits starving and dehydrating ten babies to death in neonatal unit and also it covers how cash payments to hospitals reaching their 'Death Pathway' targets may be influencing decisions. The Daily Mail to their credit also published another article on November 26th 2012 detailing how an investigation is underway to :

> "examine how hospitals have received tens of millions of pounds to implement the controversial system for care of the dying."

There are of course other options available to control the population and we'll be covering that in detail later in this book, but with headlines like:

CNCNEWS.COM August 10th 2012—"Obamacare Mandate: Sterilize 15 year old girls for free—without parental consent."

Along with statements such as:

> "Children in excess of the licensed figure will presumably be subjected to infanticide. This would be less cruel than the present method, which is to kill them by war or starvation."
> Lord Bertrand Russell, The Scientific Outlook, 1931

Are you seeing a pattern here?

Changing subject and headlines, here's one from Fox News, November 29th 2012—

"School Orders Child To Remove God From Poem"

The article explains how a six year old girl from North Carolina was ordered to remove the word 'God' from a poem she was to read on Veteran's day. The poem which honored her two grandfathers who had both fought in Vietnam was to read 'He prayed to God for peace, he prayed to God for strength'. The school explained their reason for ordering the word 'God' to be removed by saying 'We wanted to make sure we were upholding the school district's responsibility of separation of church and state from the Establishment Clause."

What happened to the Bill Of Rights with respect to Freedom of Speech and Freedom of Religion?

Would the school have done anything if the poem read 'He prayed to Satan for peace, he prayed to Satan for strength'? What is the real reason for the demise of religious expression especially that of Christianity?

In this opening chapter we have explored several headlines and subjects that really defy logic and I'm sure you'll agree that something appears be wrong in this mad, mad, mad, mad World, but is there anything linking these seemingly isolated topics together? The remainder of this book will try and provide those links. It will connect many of these isolated dots and provide you with a picture that will quickly come into focus. Please remember the golden rule of this book: If you can't believe what you are reading, put the book down, research what I have written and only continue when you have corroborated my claims.

CHAPTER 2

The Magic of Money and the Magicians Behind it

The best starting point to help in the understanding of how the pieces of the puzzle fit together and enable you to see a clear picture of what is really going on in our World is to understand the creation and manipulation of money. This subject alone can be complex and lengthy, but it is my intention to provide the basics in a simple to understand format.

Money, we all need it, and for most of us we can't get enough of it. For those who are able to amass a fortune, most will do whatever they can to maintain that status. And as we will find in this chapter some will go to extraordinary lengths to ensure that they and their offspring will maintain that wealth in perpetuity, but more importantly their power and control over all others. Would you be able to sleep at night if you knew that your deliberate and calculated actions resulted in the death of millions of people? I hope you all answer "NO!' to this, but as you will see, that cannot be said for some people who are still living or those throughout history.

Money, in the form of coinage, normally using precious metals such as gold and silver has been used for thousands of years as a method of buying and selling goods and services. It certainly solves the problem in societies that only had barter as a method of trade. Bartering is fine up until you want something from someone who doesn't want what you have to trade. The solution to this was Gold and silver coins which would be given a value based on purity and weight. Producers would then assign a value to their goods. That value would typically be based on the ease of production or availability of a product. If an ounce of spice was difficult to produce or a rare commodity then its value would increase. This also stands true for the money supply—the more money that is in supply the higher the value of goods. We shall come back to this later in this chapter, but first let's see what history can teach us.

Cleopatra who ruled over Egypt until 30 B.C. discovered something that many after her have emulated. When she found herself and Egypt in a dire economic situation with huge debts she replaced the gold and silver coinage with a much cheaper metal and forced the population to accept these new coins under the threat of death. This of course was great for her, but a debased currency and resulting high inflation was not so good for her subjects. Effectively she was able to create a great deal of money and wealth out of almost nothing. The same tactic has been used many times including during the French Revolution when the people were threatened with death and confiscation of property if they refused to accept the paper currency at face value. Snitches were rewarded for notifying authorities. Could this happen in the near future? The United States Coinage Act of 1965 diminished the silver content of the half dollar from 90% to 40%. In April 2011 Bernard von NotHaus, a sixty seven year old was labeled as a Domestic Terrorist by the F.B.I. and faces twenty five years in prison for minting his own silver coins.

Let's now look at brief example of how paper currency came into effect. Travelling through Europe and the Middle East was often a precarious undertaking and many merchants and traders found themselves being murdered or robbed for the gold or silver coins they were carrying, so to minimize this risk they looked for other options by carrying a representation of their wealth that would not be so appealing to robbers. Just like the banks of today, the Knight Templars during the Middle Ages were there to help. They had built up a network of 'banks' that enabled merchants to deposit their gold and silver in return for a paper credit note. Once they reached their destination they would exchange the credit note back to gold and silver at a local Templar 'branch' minus, of course, a small fee. The Merchant was happy and so too were the Templars who were able to build up tremendous wealth. It was a great idea but the 'banks' got greedy. They learnt that the merchants would leave their deposits for safe keeping and if they did come to make a withdrawal they rarely took out all of their money at the same time. They also started to get people coming to them asking for a loan and since they had all this money sitting there doing nothing why not lend the money out for a fee, especially since the depositors were unlikely to need it immediately?

But it didn't stop there. They learnt that they need only hold back a small percentage of depositors money in case some depositors wanted access to some of their money, whilst at the same time they could make loans using the deposits they considered to be 'in a holding pattern' and of course earn even more money in interest charges. This was the birth of Fractional Reserve Banking, a practice that is used today and a practice that has made fortunes for the bankers. Of course it doesn't come without risk. If several depositors decided to pull their gold and silver out of the 'banks' at the same time this creates a major problem for the bankers since they had loaned out more money (gold and silver) than they had in reserve—this often led to riots and the bankers being killed. Today, the bankers just call on their puppet Governments to bail them out.

Let's look at a simplistic example of Fractional Reserve Banking in today's world.

1. Bob deposits $1,000 into ABC Bank
2. By law, and using the concept of Fractional Reserve Banking, ABC Bank only needs to hold 10%, or $100 in reserve.
3. ABC Bank loans out the remaining $900 to John

4. John uses that $900 to pay Bill who fixed his truck
5. Bill takes the $900 and deposits into his bank, XYZ Bank (it could also be the same ABC Bank—it makes no difference)
6. XYZ Bank holds back 10% or $90 and loans out the remaining $810 to Ben
7. Ben uses the $810 to pay Jim for some much needed repairs to his house.
8. Jim takes the $810 and deposits into his bank.
9. Jim's bank only needs to keep $81 in reserve and loans out the rest ($729)

At this stage the banks only need to hold $271 meanwhile they have 'created' a total of $2,439 plus the original $1,000 totaling $3,439 in the system.

This process goes on and on and on and on—by now you should be starting to get the picture.

Of course in today's world of Checks and Electronic accounts there is no movement or use of gold and silver, it's just numbers on a screen. When you apply for a mortgage there's no movement of physical money from one bank to another. A clerk simply types numbers on a screen and hits 'enter'. The Banks use Fractional Reserve Banking to supply mortgages to people even though as we have seen, they do not really have the money to lend, but they certainly do make huge profits. As another simplistic example:

Joe wants to purchase a home for $220,000. He provides a 20% deposit of $44,000 and he accepts a loan from a bank of $176,000 at 3.75% over 30 years. The total interest the bank 'earns' from this loan is $117,430 plus of course the amount of the original loan which was $176,000 providing a total of $293,430

And what did the banks have to do for this? All they legally had to have in reserves was just less than $20,000, then they enter some numbers on the screen et voila. And let's not forget what happens if poor

Joe defaults on payments. The bank takes ownership of the property leaving Joe with nothing!

If there was ever a 'run on the Banks' meaning that Bob, Bill and Jim from the example above wanted to take out all of their recent deposits they would discover that the bank does not have it. This has happened many times in the past and resulted in 'Bank Holidays'—a period of time which allows the banks to call in their debts whilst being closed to depositors. A perfect example of this happened in 1907. J.P. Morgan spread a rumor that a prominent New York bank was broke. This caused all of their depositors to try and remove their money from that bank. The New York bank soon ran out of the reserves they were holding and therefore about 90% of their customers were unable to get their money out. The bank had to close while they called in the money they had loaned out. The people that had borrowed the money from the bank had to sell goods and even property to pay back the bank. When this happens in today's world, and before you dismiss such an idea I suggest you research how many banks have closed in the last ten years, we have the Federal Deposits Insurance Corporation (FDIC) to help out, but more about the FDIC later. Let's return to gold, silver and paper Credit Notes.

Up until June 5th 1933 in the United States the paper currency was backed by a measure of gold. This nullified the right of creditors to demand payment in gold. Just prior to that, in April 1933 President Franklin Delano Roosevelt ordered a confiscation of all privately held gold. Those who turned in their physical gold and certificates were given paper Dollars equal to $20.67 per ounce of gold. This gold amounting to $770 million in coins and certificates was given to the Federal Reserve. We'll look at what the Federal Reserve is later in this chapter. The following year the Government reset the value of gold to $35 per ounce therefore giving the Federal Reserve an immediate 69% percent increase in value and hence its' Balance Sheet. In 1971 President Nixon announced that they would no longer convert gold at the fixed value of $35 per ounce and by the following year the United States was completely off the 'gold standard'.

As I write this book the value of gold stands at roughly $1,700 per ounce and I'm certain this will increase as the 'Fed' increases our paper (fiat currency) money supply.

Britain had come off the gold standard in 1931.

So far we've looked at how Cleopatra forced the people of Egypt to accept coins that had no real value, we've seen how banks earn interest from money they don't really have and we've seen how the United States took gold from the ownership of its' citizens and put it into the hands of the Federal Reserve, they then significantly increased its' value, but before we take a detailed look at the Federal Reserve let's look at another typical method that is used by certain 'elite' families, let's call them 'Banksters'. These people have deliberately misled or robbed others of their wealth.

Europe 1815, the French Emperor Napoleon Bonaparte and the Anglo-Allied commander the Duke of Wellington were battling it out on the fields of Waterloo in Belgium. At that time there were no radio's or telephones with which to allow real time communications, instead speedy communications was accomplished by messengers and their horses. Nathan Rothschild's, a German Jewish banker of the Rothschild's Banking dynasty was known throughout Europe for his network of messengers and his ability to receive communications across Europe faster than most others. While taking up his normal position in the London Stock market he secretly got word from one of his messengers that Wellington had defeated Napoleon. Soon after, he began selling high volumes of stocks and bonds. Word quickly got around the Stock market and soon assumptions were being made that Rothschild's must have heard that Napoleon had triumphed since why else would he be selling. Quickly, everyone followed suit. Stocks and Bonds were sold as fast as traders could manage, leading to a total crash and collapse of stock and bond prices. Quietly Rothschild's started buying again, this time of course, stock prices and bonds were at significantly lower prices than earlier in the day. The next day official Government messengers arrived with news that it was Wellington who had won the war and not Napoleon. Loud cheers went all around and traders quickly started buying stocks and bonds again causing their value to increase, but by then Rothschild's had made an absolute fortune. The Banksters have been using this model of engineering and controlling the crashes to create panic and steal the wealth of others whilst at the same time consolidating more power into their control.

In 1910 a secret meeting was held on Jekyll Island, which is located just off the cost of Georgia. Attending this meeting were representatives of the Rothschilds', Rockefellers', J.P. Morgan, Warburg and Kuhn-Loeb—the world's leading banking families. Their agenda included: consolidate power, protect themselves from competition and create the concept of the Federal Reserve to convince everyone that it was just an agency of the government. All of this would enable them to print money out of nothing. Full details of how they achieved this can be found in G. Edward Griffins' excellent book titled "The Creature from Jekyll Island".

It took them only three years for congress to agree to the creation of the Federal Reserve—a private, run for profit Central Bank wearing the disguise of an agency of the U.S. Government. Since its creation it has never been audited and of course they have very good reasons for avoiding that.

The Federal Reserve prints money or creates money by a few keystrokes which it then loans out to other banks. Banks use these loans to provide even larger amounts of loans to their customers. If a bank makes a bad decision and too many big loans are not paid then the Federal Reserve steps in again, but this time to convince the Congress that they need to 'Bailout' the bank because they are "too big to fail" and their demise would cause major economic upheaval. In one example in the bailout of 2008 Congressman Brad Sherman stated the following on CPSAN:

"The only way they can pass this Bill is by creating and sustaining a panic atmosphere, that atmosphere is not justified. Many of us were told in private conversations, that if we voted against this Bill on Monday, that the sky would fall, the market would drop two or three points the first day, another couple of thousand the second day and a few members were even told there would be Martial Law in America if we voted 'no'. That's what I call fear mongering."

As we know in October 2008 they passed the Bill allowing for at least $700 Billion to be distributed to financial institutions who 'needed it'. And do we know who received this $700 Billion? Well, here's Senator Bernie Saunders questioning Federal Reserve chairman Ben Bernanke during a session of the Senate Budget Committee:

Sen. Sanders: "We have spent a lot of time in Congress talking about the $700 Billion T.A.R.P. bailout which I voted against as it happens. Not a whole lot has been talked about with regard to the $2.2 Trillion that the Fed has lent out. Now I find that absolutely extraordinary, that I wrote you a letter and said 'Hey who did you lend the money to? What were the terms of those loans? How can some of my constituents in Vermont get some of that money? Who makes the decisions? Do you guys sit around in a room? Do you make it? Are there conflicts of interest?' So my question to you is, will you tell the American people to whom you lent $2.2 Trillion of their dollars, will you tell us who got that money and what the terms are of those agreements?"

> Ben Bernanke: "We explain each of our programs, in terms of the terms we explain the terms exactly, we explain what the collateral requirements are, we explain . . ."
>
> Sen. Sanders: "To whom did you explain?"
>
> Ben Bernanke: "It's on our website. So all that information is available . . ."
>
> Sen. Sanders: "And who got the money?"
>
> Ben Bernanke: "Hundreds and hundreds of banks, any bank that has access to the U.S. Federal Reserve . . ."
>
> Sen. Sanders: "Can you tell us who they are?"

Ben Bernanke: "No, because the reason's that it's counter productive and will destroy the value of the program is that banks will not come to the discount window."

Sen. Sanders: "Oh isn't that too bad, in other words that's too bad, they took the money, but they don't want to be public about the fact that they received it. We heard a whole lot about A.I.G., they are on the front pages. Now I have banks and I have businesses in the State of Vermont who are in a lot of trouble, not banks, by the way our banks are doing pretty well, now how do these guys who are honest business people get it? Do you have to be a large, greedy, reckless financial institution to apply for these monies?

Ben Bernanke: "There is no subsidy, there is no capital involved, there is no gift involved, it is a collateralized short term liquid loan that is both over collateralized and is recourse to the company itself and we have never lost a penny doing it"

Sen. Sanders: "And how can other institution get those loans as well?"

Ben Bernanke: "According to the law we are supposed to be lending to depository institutions"

Sen. Sanders: "Let me just say this mister Chairman, I have a hard time understanding how you have put $2.2 Trillion at risk without making those names available, those institutions public and we're going to introduce legislation today by the way to demand that you do that. It is unacceptable to me that that goes on."

We later found out that large sums of U.S. Taxpayer money went to foreign banks. Again Senator Sanders is quoted as saying:

"We're talking about large sums of money going to bail out large foreign banks . . . . Has the Federal Reserve become the central bank of the world? I think that is a question that needs to be examined."

The Federal Reserve is nothing less than a criminal organization run primarily by foreign interests and families and as we shall see later in this book, having an huge impact on world events and the direction humanity is being taken.

Woodrow Wilson, the president who was hoodwinked into signing the Federal Reserve Act in 1913 had this to say as reported in The American Journal:

> ""I am a most unhappy man. I have unwittingly ruined my country . . . Our system of credit is concentrated. The growth of the nation, therefore, and all our activities are in the hands of a few men.
>
> We have come to be one of the worst ruled, one of the most completely controlled and dominated Governments in the civilized world—no longer a Government by free opinion, no longer a Government by conviction and the vote of the majority, but a Government by the opinion and duress of a small group of dominant men."

Woodrow Wilson was not the only President to provide such warnings after leaving office. Dwight Eisenhower's farewell address on January 17th 1961 was probably the most telling of all:

> "In the council's of government we must guard against the acquisition of unwarranted influence, whether sought or un-sought by the military industrial complex. The potential for the disastrous rise of miss-placed power exists and will persist. We must never let the weight of this combination endanger our liberties or democratic processes."

If only we had listened and taken action then.

As the money supply is pumped up with ongoing bailouts, now termed 'Quantitative Easing', the direct impact on Americans will be new direct taxes, so called 'austerity measures' and the hidden tax, inflation.

> "Inflation is the one form of taxation that can be imposed without legislation." Milton Friedman, Nobel Laureate Economist

> "The way to crush the bourgeoisie is to grind them down between the millstones of taxation and inflation"—Vladimir Lenin

A very interesting quote from the founder of the U.S.S.R. and something I will deal with in a future book. But let's take a look at a couple of examples of inflation and how they are currently squeezing us.

Gas prices in 2000 were at or even just under $1 per gallon. Today (at the time of writing) gas prices are around $3.70 per gallon, an increase of almost 400%.

Meanwhile, according to U.S. Census data the average household income in 2000 was $41,186 whereas in 2011 it was $49,103, an increase only of 19.3%.

Milk in 2000 was about $1.88 per gallon, today it's around $4.50 per gallon, an 239% increase—are you understanding why inflation is called the hidden tax?

And you surely don't need me to detail all the taxes we are currently saddled with such as income tax, sales tax, gift tax, inheritance tax, toll booth taxes, fishing license taxes, property taxes, telephone federal excise taxes, and on and on and on.

Given Lenin's quote above, perhaps our government considers us to be the bourgeoisie.

In a 2012 television interview on CNBC's 'The Kudlow Report' asked:

> "Do we all work for central bankers—is this global governance at last, is it one world, the central bankers in charge .... aren't we all just living and dying for what the central banks do?"

The response from Jim Iuorio, TJM Institutional Services Director was:

"To answer your question, we are absolutely slaves to central banks."

We have allowed the 'Banksters', the Central Banks, to fully control our politics and our society and we allow them to create wealth for themselves and steal it from everyone else. We have fallen into the trap that Thomas Jefferson feared in a letter reported to have been written to John Taylor in 1816:

> "I believe that banking institutions are more dangerous to our liberties than standing armies. If the American people ever allow private banks to control the issue of their currency, first by inflation, then by deflation, the banks and corporations that will grow up around [the banks] will deprive the people of all property until their children wake-up homeless on the continent their fathers conquered. The issuing power should be taken from the banks and restored to the people, to whom it properly belongs."—THOMAS JEFFERSON

At the time of writing the official U.S. National Debt is at $16,500,000,000,000 (that's $16.5 Trillion) and there are no signs that it will slow down, let alone reverse direction. According to U.S. Treasury Department data about $5.3 Trillion of U.S. Debt is owned by foreign countries with China owning about twenty five percent of that debt (about $1.3 Trillion), the Federal Reserve (remember this is a privately owned bank) owns about $1.66 Trillion and perhaps just as interesting is that Russia owns about $164 Billion.

Perhaps this explains the following news headlines:

The European Union Times, June 10, 2011—"China Wants to Build a 50 Square Mile City in the US"

The article details how the Chinese are looking to develop up to 30,000 acres a self sustaining community near Boise airport, in Idaho.

And it doesn't stop there. The Chinese Government owned CNOOC has recently purchased a third of Chesapeake Energy's Eagle Ford Shale project in South East Texas.

How's your Mandarin? You may need it when China calls in its loans.

这不是简单的娱乐

CHAPTER 3

Dont You Just Love a Nice War?

Consolidating wealth and power can sometimes be a slow process which can also lead to uprisings as the people revolt against increasing taxes and high inflation and so in order for the 'banksters' to expedite this process and divert attention elsewhere there's nothing better than to cook up a nice war. It also helps if they fund both sides so as to ensure they come out ahead no matter what the result. And if the war looks like it might be over too soon, how about changing things up so that the war gets extended—just think of the extra money that all sides will need to borrow to keep fighting and killing. Do you think that's crazy talk?

Let's take a look at a few examples over the last two hundred years. As we learnt earlier, Nathan Rothschild cleaned up in the Stock Market by cleverly controlling a crash and buying stocks and bonds for next to nothing, but it should be noted that while Nathan Rothschild provided funds for Wellington, it was his brother, Jacob Rothschild who was funding Napoleon. Coincidence? This author does not think so, and for good reason as we shall see.

The first American Civil War from 1861 to 1865 pitted brother against brother and resulted in the death of around 750,000 soldiers and an unknown number of civilians. If you believe that the issue of slavery was the reason for the Civil War, think again. G. Edward Griffin in his book *'The Creature from Jekyll Island'* provides the following summary:

> "The economic chaos and conflict of this period was a major cause of the Civil War. Lincoln made it clear during his public speeches that slavery was *not* the issue. The basic problem was that North and South were dependent on each other for trade. The industrialized North sold its products to the South which sold its cotton to the North. The South also had a similar trade with Europe, and that was an annoyance to the North. Europe was selling many products at lower prices, and the North was losing market share. Northern politicians passed protectionist legislation putting import duties on industrial products. This all but stopped the importation of European goods and forced the South to buy from the North at higher prices. Europe retaliated by curtailing the purchase of American cotton, That hurt the South even more. It was a classic case of legalized plunder, and the South wanted out. Meanwhile, there were powerful forces in Europe that wanted to see America embroiled in civil war."

And who helped fund both sides? The North was financed by August Belmont an agent of the Rothschilds, and the South was financed by the Erlangers' family who just happen to be relatives of the Rothschilds. Another coincidence?

Before we look into World War I and II, let's jump ahead to 1950 and the Korean War. The Korean War often referred to as the 'Forgotten War', should really have been called 'The war we were not supposed to win'. Shortly after World War II and prior to the Korean War the United States set up conditions for the Communist to take over China and thus prevent Chiang Kai-Shek from establishing a democracy by deliberately withdrawing aid and therefore allow Mao to take over. With China now under Communist control, Dean Acheson, The Secretary of State announced to the world that the U.S. would not be able to help defend Korea and Formosa (now Taiwan). Within six months of that statement the Russians, using North Koreans launched an attack on the South. A United Nations force led by General Douglas McArthur made a brilliant counter attack by landing forces at Inchon. They quickly cut off the supply lines of the North and within just a few weeks had pushed beyond the 38th Parallel. If McArthur had his way the war could have been ended with the troops returned home by Christmas, but officials in Washington did not want this. They prevented McArthur from bombing the Yalu bridge and did nothing to aid Chiang Kai-Shek from using what was left of his forces to attack the Communists. As a result hundreds of thousands of Chinese poured into North Korea pushing the U.N. troops back. The war continued until an armistice was signed on July 27th 1953. From Max Hastings book titled the Korean War he writes and quotes the following:

> "Many American career officers were deeply dismayed by the precedent Korea established: the United States had failed to fight a war to a victorious conclusion. Lieutenant General Arthur Trudeau, commanding the U.S. 7th Division, spoke of 'that odious armistice . . . when we let the Russians and the Chinese off the hook in Korea, we opened the door for their victory over the French in Vietnam. We should have let McArthur go to the Yalu and bomb the piss out of them on the other side.' 'I still feel very badly about Korea,' said Colonel Paul Freeman. 'I thought there had been a lot of unnecessary bloodletting for a stalemate.'"

In his review and commentary (The Naked Capitalist) on Carroll Quigley's 'Tragedy and Hope' W. Cleon Skousen writes:

> "Once Dr. Quigley had pointed out that the secret policy of the Establishment was to push the United States into a collectivist one-world society, it became increasingly clear why so many White House and State Department decisions played directly into the hands of the Soviet strategists"

And

> "... it was found that the U.S. Generals and Admirals had been
> deliberately prevented from winning the Korean War, even
> when there were several opportunities to do so. Little did
> Americans know that we were supposed to have lost South
> Korea. Owen Lattimore, a principle strategist for the Institute
> of Pacific Relations in the betrayal of China, had written an
> article in the New York Daily Compass, July 17, 1949, stating
> that the idea was to let South Korea fall, but not let it look as
> though we pushed her."

The Korean War resulted in approximately 1.5 to 2 million people
killed, wounded or MIA. This was a war that could have been avoided
altogether, or at least ended a lot sooner with a lot less casualties, but
it's clear that *Geopolitical games* were being played at the expense of
the people.

The Vietnam War which was triggered by the Gulf of Tonkin incident,
an event we'll discuss later, was another example of a war that was
deliberately extended to benefit the same 'gang' who profited from the
previous wars. It is widely known and accepted that U.S. Troops were
under several restrictions that hampered operations, but was is not
so commonly known is how the Rockefellars along with the Federal
Reserve and Council on Foreign Relations (CFR—an off shoot of the
Royal Institute of International Affair, out of London) influenced White
House policies to enable supplies, including weapons materials, to be
funneled through Soviet Russia to the North Vietnamese. In his ground
breaking book, 'None Dare Call it Conspiracy", released in 1972, Gary
Allen and Larry Abraham detail the following:

> "For fifty years the Federal Reserve-CRF-Rockefeller-*Insider*
> crowd has advocated and carried out policies aimed at
> increasing the power of their satellite, the Soviet Union.
> Meanwhile, America spends $75 Billion a year on defense to
> protect itself from the enemy the Insiders are building up.

What has been true of the past is even more valid today. The leader in promoting the transfer of technology and increasing aid and trade with the Communists is the Council On Foreign Relations."

On October 7, 1966 President Lyndon Johnson, a man who had appointed a C.F.R. member to virtually every strategic position in his administration, stated:

'We intend to press for legislative authority to negotiate trade agreements which could extend most favored-nation tariff treatment to European Communist states . . . We will reduce export controls on East-West trade with respect to hundreds of non-strategic items . . .'

The New York Times reported one week later on October 13, 1966:

'The United States put into effect today one of President Johnson's proposals for stimulating East-West trade by removing restrictions on the export of more than four hundred commodities to the Soviet Union and Eastern Europe . . .'

Among the categories from which the items have been selected for export relaxation are vegetables, cereals, fodder, hides, crude and manufactured rubber, pulp and waste paper, textiles and textile fibers, crude fertilizers, metal ores and scrap, petroleum, gas and derivatives, chemical compounds and products, dyes, medicines, fireworks, detergents, plastic materials, metal products and machinery, and scientific and professional instruments.'

Virtually every one of these 'non-strategic' items has a direct or indirect use in war. Later, such items as rifle cleaning compounds, electronic equipment and radar were declared 'non-strategic' and cleared for shipment to the Soviet Union. The trick simply is to declare almost everything as 'non-strategic'. A machine gun is still considered strategic and therefore may not be shipped to the Communists, but the tools for making the machine guns and the chemical to propel the bullets have been declared 'non-strategic'. Meanwhile, nearly 50,000 American have died in Vietnam. The Viet Cong and North Vietnamese receive eighty five percent of their war materials from Russia and Soviet bloc countries.

This trade agreement with the Soviets during a time of war should have been recorded as aiding and abetting an enemy and those responsible should have been held on charges of treason.

* * *

History tells us that when Archduke Francis Ferdinand of Austria was assassinated by a Serbian student it sparked off a chain reaction whereby Austro-Hungary declared war on Serbia, Germany declared war on Russia, who was allied with Serbia, followed by Great Britain declaring war on Germany after the German army invaded France and Belgium.

World War I battled on for four years and resulted in the deaths of ten million military and seven million civilians, the removal of Nicholas 2nd the Russian Czar, the creation of the League of Nations and huge debts owed by all countries to the Central Banks.

Could this war have been avoided or at least shortened? Why did the United States get involved? Let's review:

The British Royal Family at the outbreak of war and in fact up to 1917 had the surname Saxe-Coburg & Gotha. They changed their name to 'Windsor' in an attempt to hide the fact from the people that they were of German blood. King George V and Kaiser Wilhelm (William) II, who were leaders of Britain and Germany respectively, both shared the same Grandmother—Queen Victoria.

I find it beyond belief that these two cousins couldn't find some way to help avoid their *subjects* from being slaughtered on the battlefields, but I see no evidence to indicate that any attempts were made, leading me to believe that war was part of an agenda.

This theory is strengthened when you research how the United States became embroiled in this bloodbath. The sinking of the Lusitania, a British passenger ship, sailing from New York to Liverpool, killing 1,195 people including one hundred and ninety five Americans on May 7th 1915 provided the platform for Congress to declare war on Germany. Were the Germans that stupid? Why did they sink the Lusitania knowing that it would likely result in the United States joining the war? The Lusitania was part of the Cunard shipping line which was a major competitor to the shipping line owned by J.P. Morgan. It was known by Germany that the Lusitania had been converted to also carry cargo and that much of the cargo being carried was to aid Britain in the war effort. The German Embassy in the U.S. attempted to issue a warning to travelers advising them not to travel—see one advert that managed to get published.

NOTICE!

TRAVELLERS intending to embark on the Atlantic voyage are reminded that a state of war exists between Germany and her allies and Great Britian and her allies; that the zone of war includes the waters adjacent to the British Isles; that in accordance with formal notice given by the Imperial German Government, vessels flying the flag of Great Britian, or of any of her allies, are liable to destruction in those waters and that travellers sailing in the war zone on ships of Great Britian or her allies do so at their own risk.

IMPERIAL GERMAN EMBASSY,
WASHINGTON, D. C., APRIL 22, 1915.

In addition to the 1,195 people on the ship that day it has also been discovered that it was loaded with war materials including six million rounds of ammunition.

It should also be noted that the First Lord of the Admiralty, Winston Churchill, had issued orders to British ships to no longer obey German U-boat orders to stop and be searched. Instead they were to attempt to ram the U-boats. He had also ordered the removal of the Navy escort that would normally protect ships as they reached Irish waters and the Lusitania was also ordered to slow down, thus making it easier for a U-boat to engage and destroy the ship.

J.P. Morgan had acted as sales agent for British and French Bonds needed to fund the war. He also acted as purchasing agent for war materials, ensuring that he would profit even more. With Britain and France exhausted and close to defeat it was clear to Morgan that if Germany won the war he would lose hundreds of millions in useless Bonds as well as a loss of the profits he was making on the sale and purchases of war materials. The solution was obvious. If the U.S. could be pulled into the war and fight alongside the British and French the chances of an allied victory was much greater. Therefore, Morgan needed to create circumstances that resulted in a reaction from the public and politicians to call for entry into the war.

A classic example of PROBLEM, REACTION, SOLUTION.

To overcome the problem, something is needed to create a reaction such that the solution (that 'they' want) can be introduced.

As noted previously, another result of World War I was the removal of the Russian Czar. The revolt of the Russians against the tyranny of the Czar had been festering for over a decade before the outbreak of World War I. To placate them he agreed to introduce changes outlined in a document called 'The October Manifesto' whereby a constitutional government would be introduced, however with the war against Japan and with the outbreak of World War I the Czar managed to avoid putting a constitutional government in place. The Revolution fully manifested in March 1917 and a Provisional Government soon announced plans to set up a democratic, constitutional form of Government. The Provisional

Government also had no intention of pulling out of the war as they feared the Germans would destroy Russia.

It was soon after the Revolution and set up of the Provisional Government that Trotsky and Lenin arrived back in Russia, whereby using force they led the *Bolsheviks* to take over control and Communism in Russia was born. Leon Trotsky left New York in 1917 for Petrograd with $10,000 and a goal of organizing the Bolshevik take-over of the Provisional Government. In addition to this money, Leon Trotsky also carried a passport and other travel permits that enabled him to regain entry into Russia, a country he had been exiled from.

> "Historians must never forget that Woodrow Wilson, despite the efforts of the British Police, made it possible for Leon Trotsky to enter Russia with an American passport"—Jennings C. Wise, Woodrow Wilson: Disciple of Revolution.

On his journey back to Russia, the ship he was sailing on stopped at Halifax, Nova Scotia. Trotsky, his family and several others were removed from the ship and interned. It was understood by the Canadians that Trotsky's intentions were to stir up another revolution and pull Russia out of the war with Germany. In doing that the German army would then have been able to focus all their efforts on a single front where the British, American, French and Canadian forces were fighting. It has become clear that elements in the White House and London wanted Trotsky released. Telegrams reached the Canadians holding Trotsky that demanded his release. After five days of being held, Trotsky was set free to continue his journey and overthrow the Provisional Government, thus extending the war.

Similarly, Lenin was allowed to leave Switzerland (he had also been exiled from Russia) in April 1917 and enter Russia with about $5 million in Gold. His trip was made possible by Max Warburg, brother of Paul Warburg, and the German high command. Germany's reason for helping Lenin is obvious. They also knew he would work toward removing the Provisional Government and ensure Russia's withdrawal from the war.

Who provided these funds to Trotsky and Lenin? Evidence detailed in the books of Gary Allen (None Dare Call It Conspiracy) and Anthony Sutton (Wall Street and the Bolshevik Revolution) points the finger at the following: Paul and Max Warburg, Jacob Schiff, Colonel House, Alfred Milner, Harriman brothers and of course J.P Morgan, Rockefeller and the Rothschilds. The same *gang* who were directly responsible to the creation of the Federal Reserve just a few years earlier.

*   *   *

At the conclusion of World War II the number of deaths exceeded sixty Million, which at the time represented 2.5% of the worlds' population. It is well known and accepted that the Germans under the command of Adolf Hitler had to be stopped to avoid the whole of Europe being swept up, just as is it well understood and accepted that the Japanese attack on Pearl Harbor was the catalyst to bring the United States into the war. But who funded Hitler? Could the war have been shortened? And why did Japan feel the need to attack the United States and was there evidence that the attack on Pearl Harbor was expected and allowed to happen? The answers to these questions are vital to understanding the agenda of a handful of powerful families and how they are manipulating most countries of the world.

Within weeks of a surprise pact made with Joseph Stalin, Hitler's army marched into Poland without fear of Russian reprisal. Britain and France quickly declared war on Germany, which came as a surprise to Hitler as is detailed in David Irving's well documented book 'Hitler's War'. Europe was once again plunged into another devastating and long war.

"Wall Street and the Rise of Hitler" written by Anthony Sutton documents beyond any doubt that American big business provided money and vital materials for Hitler to launch and sustain the war.

Even before the war, back in 1934 General Smedley Butler testified to a Congressional committee that:

"I am here before the Congressional Committee, the highest representation of the American people under subpoena, to tell what I knew of activities which I believe was an attempt to set up a Fascist dictatorship. A plan that was outlined to me was to form an organization of veterans, to use as a club at least to intimidate the government and break down our democratic institutions. The upshot of the whole thing was that I was to lead an organization of 500,000 men which would be able to take over the functions of government."

This is important because the same 'gang' who attempted to overthrow the U.S. were also behind the funding of Hitler.

The people and companies identified in Sutton's book as aiding the Nazi's included:

American I.G Farben whose Directors included executives from Federal Reserve Bank of New York, Bank of Manhattan, Ford Motor Company and Standard Oil. I.G. Farben was the company that invented, produced and distributed Zyklon B gas which was used in the Nazi concentration camps.

Standard Oil, a Rockefeller company, provided the Nazi's with an additive called *Tetraethyl-lead*, that without it the Luftwaffe would not be able to fly.

General Electric who lists the Roosevelt family as one of its largest stockholders.

International Telephone and Telegraph whose board of Directors included representative of J.P. Morgan, Bank of America and National City.

Henry Ford as reported in the New York Times, December 20th 1922 was financing nationalist and anti-semitic movements. Henry Ford in 1938 was even awarded by Hitler with the Grand Cross of the German Eagle.

As reported in the Washington Times on October 17th 2003:

"President Bush's grandfather was a director of a bank seized by the Federal government because of its ties to a German industrialist who helped bankroll Adolf Hitler's rise to power, government documents show." Prescott Bush was one of seven directors of Union Bank Corp.

It should also not be forgotten that another powerful American company, International Business Machines (IBM) assisted the Nazi's in their efforts to exterminate Jewry. Edwin Black's bestselling book "IBM and the Holocaust" provides all the details and evidence.

The 'surprise' attack by Japan on Pearl Harbor on December 7th 1941 launched the United States into the war, but was it really a surprise? It's hard to believe that the U.S. government did not know especially when newspapers like *The Honolulu Advertiser* ran the headline "Japanese May Strike Over the Weekend!" on November 30th 1941. The question that should also be asked is—why was virtually the entire Pacific Fleet docked in Pearl Harbor? All the eggs in one basket, the perfect bait for the Japanese.

Why did the Japanese attack the U.S.? In the book 'Operation Snow' by John Koster, he provides evidence that the Communist Russians used moles within the U.S. Government to force Japan to attack. Specifically, Harry Dexter White, who was working in the treasury department and who had drafted an ultimatum to Japan that they could never agree to, thus forcing them to attack and bring the U.S. into the war. Included in the May 1941 Memorandum sent to Japan was the following demand:

> "Lease at once to the U.S. Government for 3 years such Naval vessels and airplanes as the United States selects, up to 50 per cent of Japan's Naval and air strength. Rental to be paid to be equal to 50 per cent of the original cost piece per year."

The Memorandum concluded:

> "In the event that Japan elected to reject the offer of peaceful solution under the terms herein indicated, the United States would have to shape her own policy accordingly. The first step in such policy would be a complete embargo on imports to Japan."

Japan was backed into a corner. They relied heavily on imports of oil and were never going to give up half of their navy and air strength and so came out fighting.

Historian, David Irving also provides evidence of communications prior to Pearl Harbor, between Winston Churchill and President Roosevelt which indicate Churchill had requested the U.S. to make a pre-emptive strike on Japan.

So far we have looked at how many American companies and well known names had provided funding and materials for the Nazi's and we've looked at how and why Pearl Harbor happened. Let's now look at how General George Patton was obstructed from ending the war in Europe ahead of its actual conclusion.

Shortly after the successful June 6th 1944 D-Day landings in Normandy, General George Patton and his Third Army along with General Courtney Hodge's First Army had all but encircled the German forces. All that was required was to close the loop at what was called the 'Falaise Gap', however he was ordered to halt by his superior, General Omar Bradley. To force his hand, his supply of gas was held back preventing him from ignoring Bradley and cutting off the German's escape route. Instead of bringing an end to war at that time it was allowed to continue for another year.

Patton was also prevented from leading the U.S. Third Army into Berlin ahead of Stalin's Russian Army. Much to his annoyance, Patton was ordered south, leaving the Russians to take Berlin and ultimately set up conditions for the Cold War.

It's no surprise therefore that strong evidence appears to show that Patton was assassinated as detailed in 'Target: Patton' by Robert Wilcox. Had he been allowed to live he would almost certainly have blew the whistle and detailed how the war was deliberately extended and how the Russians were given control over Eastern Europe.

* * *

On February 5th 2003 the then US Secretary of State, Colin Powell delivered a ten thousand five hundred word speech to the United Nations outlining the case for launching a ground war in Iraq. The speech focused on U.S. Intelligence reports that suggested Saddam Hussein did indeed have Weapons of Mass Destruction (WMD's) and therefore military intervention was required, all this despite the insistence from Iraqi leadership that they did not have such WMD's. On March 19th 'Operation Iraqi Freedom' was launched. Since then it's estimated that almost 1.5 Million civilians and soldiers have been killed as a direct result of the war. The official US military death toll stands at 4,488.

War *is* Hell, and I've yet to find any 'normal' person that likes the idea of going to war. So when the President of the United States uses the fact that we went to war on poor intelligence, at best, or most likely an outright lie as a joke it begs the question—Do our leaders have no empathy for others at all?

Here's what President George W. Bush said in March 2004 at a dinner event for Radio and television Correspondents:

> "Those weapons of mass destruction have got to be here somewhere . . . No, no weapons over there, maybe under here?"

This received much laughter although I suspect those laughing didn't unnecessarily lose a family member or loved one to this lie.

In the last one hundred years we've seen that most wars that have been engineered and deliberately extended resulting in the deaths of hundreds of millions of civilians and soldiers. The Communists benefited from World War I and the Bolshevik revolution. Stalin claims he triggered World War Two through his pact with Hitler and the use of *moles* in the U.S. Government to force Japan to attack Pearl Harbor. They were also allowed to take Berlin and extend Communism to Eastern Europe. Soon after the CIA replaced Chiang kai-Shek with Communist leader Mao Tse-Tung the Russians supported North Korea's invasion of South Korea and the United Nations army was prevented from ending the war and taking down Communist China. The *West* provided the Communists with vital supplies during the Vietnam War to keep that war going while at the same time restricting their own army from tactics that could have ended the war quickly. Are you seeing a pattern yet? We shall return to this towards the conclusion of this book.

CHAPTER 4

Its all in the BLOOD!

Vlad III or Vlad the Impaler, or better known as Dracula was the Prince of Wallachia, now Romania. He was a sadistic and vicious murderer who loved to torture people in the most brutal ways which included, cutting of limbs, blinding, strangulation, burning, cutting off noses and ears, mutilation of sexual organs, scalping, skinning, exposure to the elements or to wild animals and boiling alive. His nickname though came from what appears to be his favorite hobby—Death by impalement. Impalement is probably the most gruesome ways of dying. Vlad the Impaler would usually have horses attached to each of the victim's legs and a sharpened stake was gradually forced into the body. The end of the stake was usually oiled and care was taken that the stake not be too sharp, else the victim might die too rapidly from shock. Normally the stake was inserted into the body through the buttocks and was often forced through the body until it emerged from the mouth.

If I discovered that I was related to Vlad the Impaler I'm not sure it would be something I'd be proud of, but for Prince Charles it appears to be something he is very happy to admit. In a television interview he said:

"Transylvania is in my blood, The genealogy shows I am descended from Vlad the Impaler, so I do have a bit of a stake in the country."

Soon after this admission we find other reports detailing how George Bush is also related to Vlad the Impaler and so too is Dick Cheney. We also find that Barrack Obama is related to Bush and Cheney.

Researchers have proven that all of the forty four U.S. Presidents and many of those who campaigned against them, such as Mitt Romney, John McCain, John Kerry, Al Gore and Bob Dole, just to name the most recent ones, all have bloodline ties to British or European Royalty.

This is no coincidence. In the books "Guardians of the grail" by J.R. Church and Fritz Springmeiers' "Bloodlines of the Illuminati" they both detail how this *Royal Bloodline* goes back through the Hapburgs and Merovingian bloodlines to Mary Magdalene and Jesus Christ.

These 'elites' only marry within this bloodline. They often pair with distant cousins as was the case with Prince Charles and Diana to freshen up the blood, but be assured they will still stay within the Merovingian bloodline.

The research by Springmeier, Church, David Icke and Alex Jones also provide conclusive proof that most of the holders of this bloodline are Satanists. In fact, Alex Jones was able to secretly attend and film a satanic ritual at one of their gatherings at Bohemian Grove. That is something the keen researcher should check out. They have absolutely no empathy for other humans and hence why our history is filled with war and violent death.

Internet Search Term: **Alex Jones Bohemian Grove**

These Satanic worshipping elites use a pyramid structure of control and compartmentalize each group or organization within it. This enables them to control banking, military, politics, religion, business, education and health in such a way that the lower levels have no idea how they are all controlled at the top by a very small group.

They have been taught in the *Mystery Schools* that came out of Egypt and beyond and they understand the extent to how powerful the use of symbolism can be. These powerful symbols mean nothing to the un-illuminated eye and therefore these symbols can be used in plain sight. Just take a look at the dollar bill. It is loaded with symbolism, from the 'All Seeing Eye' above the pyramid to the owl in the top right corner on the front side of the bill. And it is no mistake or coincidence that the floodlights used in the recent London Olympics are shaped exactly as a pyramid with its all seeing eye. The opening and closing ceremonies of the London Olympics were covered with satanic symbolism.

It's no surprise therefore that it has finally come out that for over fifty years BBC television presenter, Jimmy Savile was part of a Satanic ring and that he was responsible for preying on at least 450 victims from aged 8 and up. It's also admitted that he once raped a twelve year old girl whilst chanting "Hail Satan" in Latin. This is the same Jimmy Savile who was enlisted by Prince Charles (British Royal Family) as a 'party organizer'. I wonder what sort of 'parties' they had.

Internet Search Term: **JIMMY SAVILE SATANIC RING**

Perhaps one of the most disturbing uses of symbolism in the last few years was that of Anubis, the ancient Egyptian god of the dead and protector of the dead as they journey into the afterlife, being paraded through many U.S. cities and London.

Internet Search Term: **ANUBIS NEW YORK**

It is now installed in Denver International Airport, which is very symbolic for those that have researched this relatively new airport.

Are these bloodlines using this symbolic act to tell us something?

As you will read later in this book, many events have been predicted ahead of time and given to us in various forms, so this is very ominous.

CHAPTER 5

The Depopulation Agenda, The New World Order Wants You Dead

The same bloodline that runs our world through deception and scientific technique has a plan for the massive depopulation of the world. Before we explore the details of this claim let's first take a look at some quotes by some of those who are working on this agenda.

"The population at large could be sterilized by infertility drugs intentionally put into the nation's drinking water or in food."—John Holdren, (Obama's Science Czar) Eco-science, Population, Resources, Environment 1977

"if voluntary birth reduction methods did not work a nation might have to resort to 'the addition of a temporary sterilant to staple food or to the water supply"—June 1972 Dr. Paul Ehrlich, Stanford University biologist and author of The Population Bomb

"The most merciful thing that a large family does to one of its infant members is to kill it." And *"Colored people are like human weeds and are to be exterminated."* Margaret Sanger, (Founder of PLANNED PARENTHOOD) 1920

"In order to stabilize the world population, we need to eliminate 350,000 people a day. It is a horrible thing to say, but it's just as bad not to say it."—Jacques Cousteau, Nov 1991 (Source: Eugenicist)

"Right Now there are just way too many people on the planet. A total world population of 250-300 million people, a 95% decline from present levels would be ideal." Ted Turner, CEO or turner Broadcasting and CNN (source: *Power & Money*, by Don McAlvany, Fall 1997, page 6)

"The Earth has a cancer and the cancer is man"—1974 Mankind at the Turning point—The 2nd report of the Club of Rome

"Perhaps by means of injections and drugs and chemicals the population could be induced to bear whatever its scientific masters may decide to be for its good."—Lord Bertrand Russell, The Scientific Outlook 1931

"I do not pretend that birth control is the only way in which population can be kept from increasing. There are others, which, one must suppose, opponents of birth control would prefer. War, as I remarked a moment ago, has hitherto been disappointing in this respect, but perhaps bacteriological war may prove more effective. If a Black Death could be spread throughout the world once every generation survivors could procreate freely without making the world too full."—Lord Bertrand Russell, The Impact of Science on Society 1952

"The world today has 6.8 B people. That's headed up to about 9 Billion. Now if we do a really great job on new vaccines, healthcare, reproductive health services, we could lower that by perhaps 10 or 15%"—Bill Gates (Source: live video TED audience 2010)

It's no coincidence that there are so many books, television shows and movies whose central theme is that of dramatic population reduction. Books such as Stephen King's 'The Stand', television shows like Discovery Channel's 'The Colony' and BBC's 'Survivors' along with films like 'I am Legend', '28 Days Later' and 'Twelve Monkey's', 'Revolution', 'The Road' and 'Children of Men' to name just a few . . . and they all imagine scenario's where the population has been reduced by over ninety percent—that means about six billion people must die without being replaced.

And to show that they really mean it, how about carving it in stone.

The Georgia Guidestones were erected on March 22nd (that's 3/22 for those of you that know about the Skull and Bones secret society) 1980, in Elbert County, Georgia, a remote area about 100 miles North East of Atlanta.

Internet Search term: **The Georgia Guidestones**

This monument is built with four 'guidestones', a center stone and a capstone. A total of twelve languages, eight modern and four ancient including Sanskrit are used. They were built to align with both the winter and summer solstices and the Equinox.

Carved into the stones are ten "Commandments' with the first being:

"Maintain humanity under 500,000,000 in perpetual balance with nature"

For this to be realized it would require a population reduction of about 93% or 6.5 Billion people, which is right in line with what most films, as detailed, 'predict' in their scenarios.

Who put them there? That remains a mystery, except the obviously false name of R.C. Christian has been provided which appears to be a reference to Christian Rosenkreuz, the supposed founder of the Rosicrucians, a secret society dating back to the 15th century.

What is the ordinary person to make of this? Given that the cost to build this would have been at least $225,000, it's clear that someone with plenty of spare money definitely wanted to make a statement.

In 1974, Henry Kissinger, the former Secretary of State wrote a paper now declassified titled 'National Security Study Memorandum 200'—Implications of worldwide population growth for U.S. Security and Overseas interests. In it he writes:

> "Policies to reduce fertility will have their main effects on total numbers only after several decades. However, if future numbers are to be kept within reasonable bounds, it is urgent that measures to reduce fertility be started and made effective in the 1970's and 1980's."

Two of the quotes provided at the start of this chapter also came from the early 1970's and both suggested that sterilants or infertility drugs could be put into food or water to help reduce population. Would they really do this without our consent? Let's put on our detective hats and start exploring raw data that should help us in our conclusions.

The chart shown in Fig. 1 shows the rapid decline in Birth Rate in the United States since 1910. The Birth Rate, that is the number of births per 1,000 population[1], in 1910 was 30, whereas we see that U.S. Birth Rate in 2010 was 14. This is a drop of 53% in 100 years. The CIA.gov world factbook now shows U.S. Birth Rate at 13.7.

---

[1]   It's important to note that some sources show Birth Rate as the number of births per 1,000 women, instead of population which can confuse the unknowing researcher.

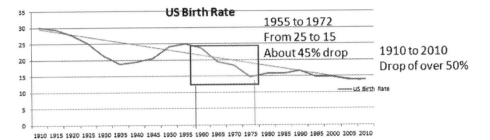

Source: 1900-1970, U.S. Public Health Service, *Vital Statistics of the United States,* annual, Vol. I and Vol II; 1971-2001, U.S. National Center for Health Statistics, *Vital Statistics of the United States,* annual; *National Vital Statistics Report* (NVSR) (formerly *Monthly Vital Statistics Report*); and unpublished data. All but most recent data compiled by *Statistical Abstract of the United States: 2008.*

Clearly the impact of wars and economic depression have had both a negative and positive impact, and I'm sure many will argue that improved contraceptives and sex education has also played its part, so let's now look at some more telling data.

In Fig.2 we see a chart that shows the Total Fertility Rate (TFR), as measured by the average number of births per woman of child bearing age.

Although this chart does not go back to 1910 you can still see a dramatic reduction, especially in the 1960's (the so called age of *free love*).

The United States now has a TFR of 2.06 according to CIA.gov which is below the recognized population replacement rate of 2.1

Fig. 2 U.S. Total Fertility Rate

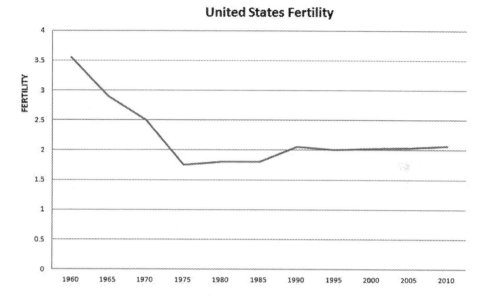

From CIA.gov we also find the following:

"Global fertility rates are in general decline and this trend is most pronounced in industrialized countries, especially Western Europe, where populations are projected to decline dramatically over the next 50 years."

Unfortunately it is not explained why Western populations are projected to decline dramatically over the next 50 years, especially since this goes completely against what we have been told for the last 20 years.

Perhaps the following news headlines will shed some light?

December 5th 2012, The Independent—Scientists Warn of Sperm Count Crisis.

"Biggest ever study confirms drastic decline in male reproductive health. Between 1989 and 2005, average sperm counts fell by a third in the study of 26,000 men, increasing their risk of infertility. The amount of healthy sperm was also reduced, by a similar proportion."

December 4th 2012, BBC News—French sperm count 'falls by a third'

"The number of millions of spermatozoa per millilitre fell by 32.3%, a rate of about 1.9% a year and the percentage of normally shaped sperm fell by 33.4%."

And the reason given?

"We still do not know which are the most important factors but the most likely are . . . a high-fat diet and environmental chemical exposures."

Similarly, another study reported:

Mail Online, January 31, 2013—"Sperm Quality has declined by 38% in a decade—and poor diet and lifestyle could be to blame'

This article details that "even in young men, sperm concentrations fell by an average of two percent every year."

What is really behind this dramatic drop in sperm count and why are we being told the scientists don't know the reason? Here's a few more news headlines from scientists that do seem to know.

October 28th 2010, The Telegraph, Bisphenol—A now linked to male infertility.

"A controversial chemical used for decades in the mass production of food containers and baby bottles has been linked to male infertility for the first time.

Bisphenol-A (BPA), known as the "gender bending" chemical because of its connection to male impotence, has now been shown to decrease sperm mobility and quality.

BPA is used widely to make plastic harder and watertight tin cans. It is found in most food and drink cans—including tins of infant formula milk—plastic food containers, and the casings of mobile phones, and other electronic goods."

August 5th 2010, 'Gender Bending' chemical found in food tins may cut male fertility.

"A 'gender bending' chemical in food and drinks containers could be behind rising male infertility, scientists say.

Men with high levels of Bisphenol A (BPA) in their bodies are more likely to have low sperm counts, according to a study.

The chemical mimics the female sex hormone estrogen and interferes with the way hormones are processed by the body . . . . Scientists have now discovered it could be lined to poor sperm quality and concentration."

Ten days later on August 15th 2010 the same news paper has the headlines:

Gender-bending chemical found in tin cans and shop receipts 'can cause fatal clogging of arteries'

"A gender-bending chemical found in sunglasses, baked bean cans and shop receipts fuels potentially fatal narrowing of the arteries, research suggests.

The study of British men and women found a clear link between high levels of bisphenol A and the clogging up of the arteries the provide the heart with oxygen-rich blood.

Coronary heart disease is Britain's biggest killer, claiming almost 100,000 lives a year by triggering heart attacks and other problems."

March 4, 2011, BBC News—Cancer rates rise and sperm quality falls 'Due to chemicals'

"Sperm quality significantly deteriorated and testicular cancers increased over recent years, a Finnish study says.

"The study in the International Journal of Andrology looked at men born between 1979 and 1987 . . . Total sperm counts were 227m for men born in 1979-81, 202m for those born in 1982-83 and 165m for men born in 1987, respectively . . . . The fact that sperm counts have dropped so quickly, and mirrors the increase in the incidence of testicular cancer in Finland, suggests that the effect is probably environmental."

December 1ˢᵗ 2011, The Daily Mail—Radiation from WiFi connections can reduce sperm activity in up to a quarter of men, study finds"

"Working on a laptop wirelessly may hamper a man's chances of fatherhood.
In a study, sperm placed under a laptop connected to the internet through wi-fi suffered more damage than that kept at the same temperature but away from the wireless signal. In the latest study, researchers took sperm from 29 men aged 26 to 45 and placed them either under a wi-fi connected laptop or away from the computer."

The article continued to detail how in experiment, 25 per cent of sperm under the laptop had stopped moving and 9 per cent showed DNA damage, compared to just 14 per cent of samples kept away from the wi-fi stopped moving.

It seems strange to me that in 2010 and 2011 we are presented with news and scientific evidence that male fertility is being affected by chemicals found in our food and water containers, the ink used on shop receipts and radiation from Wi-Fi's and yet in 2012 we have 'scientists' telling us that they don't know why the sperm count has dropped so much.

I do not believe you need to be a "Columbo" to work this out.

Whilst researching experiments carried out by Nazi scientists during World War II, I came across the following transcript taken from the Nuremburg Trials and made available by the Harvard Law School Library.

In a letter to Heinrich Himmler (head of Nazi SS) describing methods of mass sterilization, Viktor Hermann Brack in 1941 writes:

1. "One way to carry out these experiments in practice would be to have those people who are to be treated line up before a counter. There they would be questioned and a form would be given them to be filled out, the whole process taking two or three minutes. The official attendant who sits behind the counter can operate the apparatus in such a manner that he works a switch [that] will start both tubes together (as the rays have to come from both sides)." (Source: Harvard Law School Library—Nuremberg Trials Project)

Brack believed that one installation with two tubes would allow 150 to 200 persons to be sterilized daily and with 20 installations they would sterilize 3,000 to 4,000 persons daily.

In this same report the defendant, Brack explained that the latest X Ray technology enabled mass sterilization without the victims finding out.

Perhaps most of the governments around the world are not aware of the Nazi experiments and their plans to use X Rays for mass sterilization—or perhaps they are.

Everyone knows that when you have an X Ray at the doctors or dentists your vital organs are shielded by lead, but when you go through the airport security backscatter machines that are delivering significantly higher doses of radiation than the Nazi's were using, you have no protection at all.

A quick digression. What was the catalyst for billions of tax payer dollars to be spent on such powerful X Ray machines? Answer: it was the so called underwear bomber of Christmas 2009 who attempted to blow up a plane in mid air using explosives concealed in his underwear. Michael Chertoff, who was head of Department of Homeland Security at the time made the compelling case for spending the money mostly with Rapiscan Systems, a company that was a client of his Chertoff Group company. But we discover that Kurt Haskell, a passenger on that plane testified under oath that he witnessed the underwear bomber being escorted around security by a man in a tan suit in Amsterdam where the plane took off.

(Source: Fox 2 News, Detroit)

Let's return to the headline that exposed the damage that laptop Wi-Fi radiation does to male infertility. If radiation from a laptop can have such a devastating effect on sperm count what about the radiation that bombards us every day from cell phone towers, Wi-Fi routers and let's not forget the huge amounts of radiation being emitted from the new 'Smart Meters' that are being installed at almost every home. Are we going to be surprised to read in the next decade that sperm count has fallen to critical levels but scientists say it's not known why. I suggest that those who funded the Georgia Guidestones will not be at all surprised.

In the earlier quotes from Russell, Holdren and Ehrlich they suggested that a sterilant could be put into the food and water supply to reduce the population.

Renowned chemist Charles Perkins who was sent from Washington to take charge of the German Nazi IG Farben chemical plant at the end of World War II and who reported on the use of Fluoride experiments carried out in Auschwitz and other concentration camps stated:

> "Even in small quantities, sodium fluoride is a deadly poison to which no effective antidote has been found. Every exterminator know that it is the most efficient rat-killer"

He also went on to say:

> "*I say this in all earnestness and sincerity of a scientist who has spent the last twenty years doing research into chemistry, bio-chemistry, physiology and the pathology of fluorine: Any person who drinks artificially fluoridated water for a period of one year or more will never again be the same person mentally or physically.*"

The Nazis were not the first to use or experiment with and Fluoride. Stalin's regime used fluoride in the prison water supply from the 1930s as a tranquilizer. This was when the idea was exported to Britain.

In a testimony to the government in the Hearing before a special committee on Un-American Activities Report to seventy sixth Congress in 1939 it was revealed that Communist sympathizers in the US has discussed using fluoride to make the population docile while they brought in Communism by degrees in the US upon a lethargic population.

> "while a member of the Communist Party, I attended Communist training schools in New York and Wisconsin . . . we were trained in the revolutionary overthrow of the US Government. We discussed quite thoroughly the fluoridation of water supplies and how we were using it in Russia as a tranquilizer in the prison camps. The leaders of our school felt that it could be introduced into the American water supply, it would bring about a spirit of lethargy in the nation, where it could keep the general public docile during a steady encroachment of Communism. We also discussed the fact that keeping a store of deadly fluoride near the water reservoir would be advantageous during the time of the revolution, as it would give us opportunity to dump this poison into the water supply and either kill off the populace or threaten them with liquidation, so that they would surrender to obtain fresh water."

And from

HEARINGS BEFORE THE COMMITTEE ON INTERSTATE AND FOREIGN COMMERCE HOUSE OF REPRESENTATIVES EIGHTY-THIRD CONGRESS SECOND SESSION ON H. R. 2341 A BILL TO PROTECT THE PUBLIC HEALTH FROM THE DANGERS OF FLUORINATION OF WATER—

MAY 25, 26, AND 27, 1954

"I have stated repeatedly—and I reiterate—that anyone who has anything to do for fluoridation, is displaying a treacherous attitude for one of four reasons—either because he is uninformed, misinformed, dishonest, or subversive. Unquestionably, practically everything in this Nation is infiltrated by Communists, subversives, and their dupes or tools.

Seventeen million Americans, more or less, at the mercy of Soviet Communists. Invasion and sabotage, by remote control, through the water mains. What could be more clever or effective? Our enemies take over—city by city.

I know that fluoridation is a Communist scheme—frankly, the master plan—but I cannot prove it, for those who have informed me, cannot testify—they would be liquidated, if they did. I believe you are in a position to prove it, however, by having Princess Ileana and others testify under oath.

The catalyzing of water fluoridation is being successful and millions of American are being poisoned. I also believe that a Federal law should be quickly passed to prohibit this scheme, in order to avert further diseasing and perhaps killings of our innocent and protesting citizens—and to prevent the complete loss of faith in this administration which so many are experiencing."

On July 21st 1976 Dr. Dean Burke Ph.D wrote a Congressional Recorded that stated:

"In point of fact, Fluoride causes more human cancer death, and causes it faster than any other chemical"

In the U.K. Poisons Act of 1972 Fluoride is detailed as a Class 2 poison under the names—

Hydrofluoric acid

#Alkali metal bifluorides

#Ammonium bifluoride

#Alkali metal fluorides

#Ammonium fluoride

Sodium silicofluoride

Hence why our toothpaste carries the following warning:

> "Keep out of reach of children under 6 years of age. If more than used for brushing is accidently swallowed, get medical help or contact a Poison Control Center right away"

Some products such as 'Colegate Prevident' now contains 5,000 parts per million (PPM) and yet scientists have proven that just 1 PPM can be devastating as reported in the following:

June 21 2011, PR Newswire—New Study: Fluoride Can Damage the Brain—Avoid Use in Children

> "Fluoride can be toxic by ingesting one part per million (ppm), and the effects are not immediate, as they can take 20 years or more to become evident"

And:

July 20 2012, U.S. National Library of Medicine—Developmental Fluoride Neurotoxicity: A systematic review and Meta Analysis

> "Children in high fluoride areas had significantly lower IQ scores than those who lived in low fluoride areas."

In addition to being a known poison, lowering IQ and a major cause of cancer, Fluoride is also been identified as calcifying the pineal gland (it's important that you research what the pineal gland does), a sterilant and is the main ingredient found any most anti-depressant drugs.

One of the worlds' leading producers of Fluoride based in Yunnan, China provides the following details on their website:

> "Sodium Fluoride—Uses: it is used in the manufacture of effervescing steel, and the smelting and refining of light metals. It is also used in fluorination of drinking water, as a wood preservative, an adhesive preservative. An insecticide, a protective coating for metals, a pickle for steels and other metals, a flux for soldering and welding, as well as a flux and pacifier for ceramic, glass and porcelain enamel."

> (Source: http://www.imexbb.com/sodium-silicofluoride-sodium-fluosilicate-sodium-fluoride-watertreatment-10781815.htm)

Despite all of this we allow our water supply to be 'treated' with Fluoride to "help prevent dental decay". Are you getting the picture yet?

In the towns and cities that I live closest to, the water districts proudly show that Fluoride is added with between 4 PPM and 7 PPM. But that's not all that's added. Again, just for the two water districts near me they also add Sodium Hyperchlorite or Chloramine. These are both listed as poisons and are especially dangerous when fumes from these substances are breathed in. Think about that the next time you take a shower and breath in the fumes that the shower head produces.

This method of slowly poisoning us is often referred to as a *Soft Kill*. You may not feel the effects of these poisons immediately, but over time they are devastating. Much of the world is being deliberately *Soft Killed* by the food we eat, the water we drink and other everyday sources. But there are some devices that are being used on us that are not so *soft*.

Remember Bill Gates' quote

> "The world today has 6.8 B people. That's headed up to about 9 Billion. Now if we do a really great job on new vaccines, healthcare, reproductive health services, we could lower that by perhaps 10 or 15%"

And another from Lord Bertrand Russell:

> "Diet, injections, and injunctions will combine, from a very early age, to produce the sort of character and the sort of beliefs that the authorities consider desirable, and any serious criticism of the powers that be will become psychologically impossible."—The Impact of Science on Society p 62

If you haven't figured out the link, here's a few more clues:

March 11, 2004 UNICEF Nigerian Polio Vaccine Contaminated with Sterilizing Agents Scientist Finds

"A UNICEF campaign to vaccinate Nigeria's youth against polio may have been a front for sterilizing the nation. Dr. Haruna Kaita, a pharmaceutical scientist and Dean of the Faculty of Pharmaceutical Sciences of Ahmadu Bello University in Zaria, took samples of the vaccine to labs in India for analysis

Upon analysis, found evidence of serious contamination. "Some of the things we discovered in the vaccines are harmful, toxic; some have direct effects on the human reproductive system," he said in an interview with Kaduna's Weekly Trust. "I and some other professional colleagues who are Indians who were in the Lab could not believe the discovery,'"

December 20, 2012, NBC News—Rumors of plot to sterilize Muslims with polio vaccine sparks killing in Pakistan

"Pakistan may be one of the world's three remaining polio-stricken countries but Sartaj Khan has decided that the government-sponsored vaccination campaign is much more sinister than it appears. These vaccines are meant to destroy our nation," said Khan, a 42-year-old lawyer in the city of Peshawar. "The [polio] drops make men less manly, and make women more excited and less bashful. Our enemies want to wipe us out."

January 23, 2013 Natural News.com—"At Least 50 African children paralyzed after receiving Bill Gates—backed meningitis vaccine"

"Bill and Melinda Gates have been on a crusade for at least the past decade to vaccinate every single child on the planet. And one of their primary geographical targets has been the continent of Africa, where poor sanitations and lack of clean water have created conditions in which diseases like meningitis and malaria run rampant. But rather than try to meet these basic needs, the multi-billionaires and their many allies have instead thrust vaccines on indigenous populations as the solution, which has in turn sparked a wave of paralysis among Africa's younger populations."

In the past, vaccines have helped prevent disease, but as we have seen they can also be used for much more sinister plans and why Russell and Gates suggest that vaccines can be used to reduce populations. Here's just a few typical vaccine ingredients:

Thimerosal: A neurotoxic mercury which causes autism: There are 25 mcg in one average flu vaccine, and the EPA safety limit is 5 micrograms, so children who are vaccinated simultaneously with multiple vaccines receive over ten times the safety limit of mercury in one day.

Polysorbate 80: is 'valued' for its ability to produce infertility in animals. Polysorbate 80 is known to cause anaphylactic shock.

Bovine Cow Serum: Extracted from cow skin. When injected causes connective tissue disorders, arthritis and lupus; also shortness of breath, low blood pressure, chest pain and skin reactions.

Formaldehyde: Highly carcinogenic fluid used to embalm corpses. Ranked one of the most hazardous compounds to human health; can cause liver damage, gastrointestinal issues, reproductive deformation, respiratory distress and cancer.

Squalene/MF59: is a sub-micron oil-in-water emulsion of a squalene, polyoxyethylene sorbitan monooleate (TweenTM 80) and sorbitan trioleate. Squalene is also a natural substance found in the brain, so when injected and attacked by the body's immune system it then attacks the naturally occurring squalene which many suggest leads to Guillain Barre Syndrome.

SV40: Simian vacuolating virus 40 or *Simian virus 40*,: a polyomavirus that is found in both monkeys and humans. Like other polyomaviruses, SV40 is a DNA Virus that has the potential to cause tumors, but most often persists as a latent infection.

Dr. Maurice Helleman, a scientists working for Merck admitted that SV40 known as a cancer virus was found, along with 39 other viruses in the Polio vaccine. Dr. Helleman and the interviewer both laugh at that fact.

I know, that's just too much to believe, well if the internet and Youtube is still available I suggest you search and watch for yourself.

Internet Search term: **'Maurice Helleman SV40'.**

When you hear of healthworkers and/or the general public being forced to take a vaccine(s) then that, I suggest, is something you do your best to avoid.

I suggest that the keen researcher also looks into the impact that Genetically Modified foods and other chemically produced food substances such as Aspartame, high fructose corn syrup and monosodium Glutamate (MSG) are having on our bodies and working in conjunction with a planned depopulation agenda. Conversely, I suggest the researcher explores the benefits of pure and natural foods such as raw & non pasteurized milk, raw honey, hemp and other incredibly beneficial foods and minerals which are being demonized and indeed some cases being criminalized by our governments and mainstream media. When researching GMO foods try to answer this question: Why is it that the Food and Drug Administration (FDA) is forbidden from examining the safety of GMO foods other then reviewing the safety reports puts provided by companies like Monsanto that holds the GM patents? Do you really think we should put all our trust in Monsanto and others?

There are of course some that aren't patient enough for the *soft kill* agenda to work its magic. Some like Dr Erik Pianca, American Biologist openly called for a mass genocide of 90% of the worlds' population. At a speech given to the Texas Academy of Science in March 2006 he exclaimed that:

"we are no better than bacteria"

And he went on to advocate the release of airborne ebola virus as his preferred method of exterminating 90% of humans.

Perhaps this might also explain the following headlines:

May 3, 2012, The Daily Mail—It's out there: Science Journal publishes details of deadly lab made bird flu that 'could cause global pandemic'

> "The science journal Nature has published the first of two controversial papers about laboratory-enhanced versions of the deadly bird flu virus—described by some as a 'recipe' for a bioterror attack.
>
> The virus sparked fears among U.S. biosecurity experts that it could be used as a recipe for a bioterrorist attack."

And:

November 28, 2011, The Daily Mail—Anthrax isn't scary at all compared to this': Man-made flu virus with potential to wipe out many millions if it ever escaped is created in research lab

> "A group of scientists is pushing to publish research about how they created a man-made flu virus that could potentially wipe out civilization."

Humanity is being attacked on all fronts with the end goal of massive depopulation and they are well on target. If we are to avoid a "Children of Men" scenario (if you are not familiar with this movie, I suggest you watch it, but in summary it's based in 2027 and 18 years since the last baby was born) action needs to be taken now.

Of course you will not find the "elite bloodlines" taking vaccines, drinking fluoridated water or eating GMO foods. That is just for the *useless eaters*.

Dr. Rima Laibow M.D. and Medical Director of the Natural Solutions Foundation, puts it very succinctly in a December 2012 interview:

"There is a genocidal depopulation agenda, which I call a war against the population of the earth. The World Health Organization, the United States Government, the Council on Foreign Relations, the United Nations and many other similar organizations have joined together in a shared vision. It's a wonderful vision. It's the vision of a sustainable planet, there will be blue skies everywhere, there will be clean water running everywhere, there will be green grass and cows peacefully in the distance, and you and I and our children and our children's children will no longer exist. We will not be there to appreciate this beautiful sustainable world, because we would have been eliminated by the *elite*, by the *globalists*. Since we, in their vision are 'useless eaters'. 'Useless eaters', their term of art for us. We, they say consume their non-renewable natural resources. We, they say are not needed for what they call the neo feudal world. As which was explained to me by a head of State who was my patient and who told me this in my office. There will be a small circle of neo aristocrats at the top surrounded by their servants and servitors who are in turn surrounded by their technicians. Which takes about ten per cent of the current world population, everyone else she said will be culled. C, U, L, L, E, D."

Let's finish this chapter with another quote from Lord Bertrand Russell's 1931 book 'The Scientific Outlook'

"Just as the sun worship of the Aztecs demanded the painful death of thousands of human beings annually, so the new scientific religion will demand its holocaust of sacred victims."

CHAPTER 6

Moving Along with the Agenda

For hundreds of years well funded scientists have been studying humans. How the human body works, how mind works and how humans react under certain conditions. Wartime offers tremendous freedom for experiments that would otherwise be impossible to perform. Whether it be experiments carried out on the Jews during World War II or experiments carried out on soldiers such as exposure to radiation also during World War II, or Agent Orange during Vietnam, or 'trial' vaccines given to Marines during the first Gulf War. Other experiments or 'trial balloons' are carried out in a more subtle ways. One such example was holding back supplies of food and water during the Haiti earthquake or hurricane Katrina. These are typically explained away as incompetence on behalf of certain people or organizations, but be assured they are deliberate and provide vital data to help their agenda. For example: how long will people last without food and water before they allow their guns to be confiscated, how long before people will ask to be taken away and put into 'survival centers' or FEMA camps and, in the case of Haiti earthquake, how long before people start hacking each other to death with machetes for food.

This scientific understanding allows them to move their agenda along in such a way that the vast majority of the people are ignorant of what is really going on and to such an extent that anyone from the small percentage of people that are *awake* are ridiculed or dismissed as being a *crazy conspiracy theorist*. Sound familiar?

They use several scientifically proven techniques to move their agenda along without causing the majority to wake up and revolt.

1. Step by Step—or Fabian Socialism a term coined from Fabius Cunctator, also known as Fabius the delayer was a Roman General who preferred gradualism over revolution. Taking time to change perceptions and behaviors rather than pitched battles. Renowned author and researcher David Icke calls it the "Totalitarian Tip Toe". Taking small steps to push humanity along a path that couldn't be done by taking big steps. A small tax here, another new law and tax there and so on until one day you look back and wonder "how on earth did we allow ourselves to get to this point?"

2. Keeping you busy—it's no *accident* that we have sports events that last for 3 hours a day or more and take up almost all of our 'free' time. It's also no accident that Doctors and others such as the Police are expected and required to work so many hours. This makes it very difficult for them to take the time to properly research the latest drugs or laws, that had they done so might make them suspicious of real reasons.

3. Predictive Programming—as Bertrand Russell stated back in 1931 "the producers of Hollywood are the new high priests". By using Television and movies to subconsciously plant

thoughts and ideas into the mind of the watcher they are able to manipulate the people to change their behaviors according to the programming. Using their *Depopulation Agenda* as an example: just think of the hundreds of television shows and movies that depict a world that has been decimated leaving our *heroes* to survive a post apocalyptic world. Or how the idea of 'man made global warming' is pushed. A perfect example of this can be found in the popular television series "Northern Exposure" in which one episode titled 'Survival of the Species' from 1993 include three such classic examples. In one scene, a future dream sequence, the character Shelly takes off her raincoat and announces that it cost twenty five "energy units". Later another character talking of how the world would be slowly destroyed says "the human mind, it doesn't think in geological increments . . . the reality is even at current rates of environmental destruction it'll take considerable time for our species to disappear. Sure there will be famine, riots and plagues, but most people will go on as they always have, ignoring and adapting, until finally the planet truly is uninhabitable." In the last example from the same episode the character, Ed, says the following "The average American citizen dumps 3,000 pounds of trash every year. Just seems like the only thing left to do if you're a responsible citizen is to kill yourself." Once you know what to look for you will start seeing similar 'programming' in almost every television show and movie. Before the rather sudden and globally coordinated move to HD Television we had televisions whose frequency range operated at between 50-60 hz, which was in line with the human brain and thus helped put the watcher into a trance like state. Given the change to HD, you certainly have to wonder what they are able to do using HD. I can guarantee it is not for your benefit.

4. Education—again, in the words of Bertrand Russell "Education has two purposes; on the one hand to form the mind, on the other hand to train the citizen." Our children are being pushed into schools at an early age to get them indoctrinated and

brainwashed into ensuring that they follow the "program". Any child that shows too much energy or asks too many questions are quickly diagnosed with Attention Deficit Hyperactivity Disorder (ADHD) and drugged to repress them. In David Icke's book "Remember Who You Are" he details how Dr. Richard Day in 1969 spoke of the agenda of the 'New World Order' and how they planned to use schools as a tool of indoctrination, how children would spend more time in school but wouldn't learn anything. Our children are being trained to remember and repeat, they are not being taught to think. Anyone who tries to help their child with mathematics homework will likely find it a struggle. The way math was taught twenty to thirty years ago is very different to how it's taught now, making it difficult for the caring parent to help their child, and this is done deliberately in an attempt to break the bond between child and parent. The child soon learns that they can only get help from their teachers and that their parents are of no help—this is a prime example of how they are being manipulated.

5. Control of the media—In a speech given by David Rockefeller at a Bilderberg Meeting in 1991 he said:

> "We are grateful to *The Washington Post*, *The New York Times*, *Time* magazine, and other great publications whose directors have attended our meetings and respected their promise of discretion for almost forty years. It would have been impossible for us to develop our plan for the world if we had been subject to the bright lights of publicity during those years."

Controlling hundreds of media outlets would be an impossible task, but controlling half a dozen companies is a lot easier. And this is exactly what has happened. According to Business Insider 90% of American Media in 1983 was owned by 50 companies. In 2011 90% of companies were owned by just 6 companies. These are: General Electric (NBC, Comcast & Universal Pictures),

Newscorp (Fox News, Sky News, Wall Street Journal & NY Post), Disney (ABC, ESPN, Pixar, Miramax), Viacom (CMT, MTV, BET, Paramount), Time Warner (CNN, Time, HBO & Warner Bros.) and CBS (Showtime, 60 minutes). They have control over TV Shows, News (TV and print), movies and radio. Compare this to the list of attendees at the secretive Bilderberg Meetings that are held every year and you will find executives from every one of these companies in attendance.

6. Divide & Rule and political control—Carroll Quigley in his 1300 page monster of a book, Tragedy & Hope, that details the history of the world and in particular the founding of the Royal Institute of International Affairs and the Council of Foreign Relations explains how these shadow groups have been controlling both sides of the political spectrum for the last sixty years. Tragedy & Hope was published in 1962. We are given *players* to vote for. They appear sincere and might argue with their counterparts, but they are merely acting their parts. They take their orders from higher up in the *Shadow Governments*.

    Hillary Clinton in a speech at the Council on Foreign Relations on July 15 2009 said the following: "It's good to have an outpost of the Council (CFR) right here down the street from the State Department. We get a lot of advice from the Council, so it means I won't have that far to go to be told what we should be doing and what we should think about the future" Democrats are pitted against Republicans, religious groups are set against each other and even some "conspiracy" theorists are pitted against each other in a Machiavellian technique to get two or more parties fighting with each other, unaware they both are being controlled and manipulated. We described an example of this earlier with Stalin during World War II.

7. False Flags or staged events—For thousands of years the use of False Flag events, that is, staging an event and blaming it on another party to create a reaction that supports the agenda

of the false flag creators, has been a most favored tool for manipulating people especially when a big change is required.

Before we examine a few False Flag events in more detail it is worth pointing out that in W. Cleon Skousen's book "The Naked Communist" published in 1958 he details a forty five point plan of stated Communist goals. These included:

- Develop the illusion that total disarmament by the United States would be a demonstration of moral strength.
- Promote the United Nations as the only hope for mankind.
- Capture one or both of the political parties in the United States
- Get control of the schools . . . Soften the curriculum . . . Put the party line in textbooks.
- Infiltrate the press . . .
- Gain control of key positions in radio, TV and motion pictures.
- Break down cultural standards of morality by promoting pornography and obscenity in books, magazines, motion pictures, radio and TV.
- Present homo-sexuality, degeneracy and promiscuity as 'normal, natural, healthy'.
- Infiltrate the churches and replace revealed religion with 'social' religion.
- Discredit the American Constitution by calling it inadequate, old-fashioned, out of step with modern needs . . .
- Discredit the American founding fathers.
- Support any socialist movement to give centralized control over any part of culture—education, social agencies, welfare programs, mental health clinics, etc.
- Discredit the family as an institution. Encourage promiscuity and easy divorce.
- Internationalize the Panama Canal

I'd say they look to be scoring very high marks.

Headline from 'The Blaze' January 26, 2103 "**PIERS MORGAN: BOTH THE BIBLE AND U.S. CONSTITUTION ARE 'INHERENTLY FLAWED' AND NEED TO BE AMENDED"**

It begs the question: is Piers Morgan working for the Commies? Hopefully the answer to that will become clear at the end of this book.

Let's now return to look at a few False Flag events that have created big changes in our world.

In the early 1930's the Communist Party and National Socialist (Nazi) party were virtually equal in popularity, but on February 27th 1933 the fire at the Reichstag (Germany's Parliament) in Berlin, enabled Adolf Hitler and his National Socialist, Nazi, party to take over. A retarded, almost naked Dutch youth named Marinus van der Lubbe was caught and said to have been carrying a Communists Party card. Although after interrogation he confessed to starting the fire it later came out that it would have been impossible for him to have acted alone and that the incendiary devices had to have been carried via a tunnel that led to Hermann Goering's office, one of Hitler's closest partners. The Nazi party acted quickly to bring down the Communist party and also used the fire to introduce the "Enabling Act" which allowed racial profiling, gun confiscation and issuance of national identity cards.

The Gulf of Tonkin resolution that passed the U.S, Congress on August 7th 1964 led directly to a declaration of war which as described earlier in this book and resulted in over a million people killed. This resolution was based on an alleged attack by the North Vietnamese on the U.S. Navy destroyers Maddox and Turner Joy in the Gulf of Tonkin on August 4th 1964. The Turner Joy then fired 220 rounds at ground targets in North Vietnam. In November 2001 the LBJ presidential library and museum released tapes in which the President and Secretary of Defense openly discuss plans to stage an incident as a pretext to expand the war.

In 2005 a declassified National Security Agency report stated:

"It is not simply that there is a different story as to what happened; it is that no attack {on the U.S. Navy} happened that night."

Operation Ajax in 1953 as described by the CIA on their official website (CIA.gov) was "an American Coup". It was designed to remove the democratically elected leader Mohammad Mossadeq of Iran and replace him with a *puppet* Shah. It details how they (the CIA) "carried out its first successful regime change operation" by:

> "The plan comprised propaganda, provocations, demonstrations, and bribery, and employed agents of influence, "false flag" operatives, dissident military leaders, and paid protestors. The measure of success seemed easy enough to gauge—all that really mattered was that Tehran be in turmoil,"

And why did the U.S. conduct this regime change? Because Mossadeq nationalized the Anglo Iranian Oil Company. CIA.gov states:

> "Britain's new prime minster, Winston Churchill, was committed to stopping his country's empire from unraveling further."

Is anyone taking notes here? Winston Churchill who was First Lord of the Admiralty during World War I and removed the destroyer escort from the Lusitania which ultimately led to U.S. intervention, and who helped ensure Stalin could take Berlin at the end of World War II and therefore set up conditions for the Cold War, didn't like his buddies in the oil industry losing out on billions of dollars and so he called in some favors from the U.S.

I suggest the really keen researcher reads some of the writings of the great historical author, David Irving, in particular 'Churchill's War', to learn some hard truth about *Winnie, the British Bulldog.*

There are so many more examples of False Flag events such as Operation Gladio, the attacks on the U.S.S. Liberty and the Mumbai Massacre to name just a few, but let's just look at a few more well documented examples.

Operation Northwoods, now declassified and reported in ABC News in May 2001 details how in 1962

> "U.S. top military leaders drafted plans to kill innocent people and commit acts of terrorism in U.S. cities to create public support for a war on Cuba."

The plan included sinking Cuban refugee boats, hijacking planes, blowing up a U.S. ship and even conducting acts of terrorism in U.S. Cities. Documents show the Joint Chiefs even proposed using the potential death of astronaut John Glenn during the first attempt to put an American into orbit as a false pretext for war with Cuba. Should the rocket explode and kill Glenn, they wrote, "the objective is to provide irrevocable proof . . . that the fault lies with the Communists et al Cuba. [sic]"

The plans had the written approval of all of the Joint Chiefs of Staff and were presented to President Kennedy's defense secretary, Robert McNamara, in March 1962. John F. Kennedy did not approve this plan.

Investigative reporter James Bamford wrote the following:

> "The whole point of a democracy is to have leaders responding to the public will, and here this is the complete reverse, the military trying to trick the American people into a war that they want but that nobody else wants."

The 1993 bombing of the World Trade Center, a Ryder truck filled with explosives failed to bring down the North Tower but did kill six people and injured over a thousand. The New York Times published an article in October 28th 1993 with the headlines:

"Tapes Depict Proposal to Thwart Bomb Used in Trade Center Blast"

In this article it describes how secret tapes recorded by Emad Salem showed that the F.B.I. knew of a bomb threat and instead of removing the explosives they insisted that live explosives be used and allowed to detonate.

Internet search term: **NY TIMES TAPES DEPICT PROPOSAL**

The article details how the FBI knew of plans to blow up the World Trade Center and that they were to thwart the plot by secretly substituting harmless powder for the explosives, but an FBI supervisor called off that plan, therefore allowing the bombing to go ahead. Emad Salem a 43 year old former Egyptian army officer was being used by the U.S. Government to penetrate a group of Muslim extremists, but after believing he was being setup he began to record conversation with his FBI handlers. Hundreds of hours of these recordings were presented to the court. The recordings proved that Salem wanted to complain to FBI headquarters about the failure to stop the bombing, but that he was dissuaded from doing so by an agent identified as John Anticev. The NY Times article includes the following:

> "Do you deny," Mr. Salem says he told the other agent, "your supervisor is the main reason of bombing the World Trade Center?" Mr. Salem said Mr. Anticev did not deny it. "We was handling the case perfectly well until the supervisor came and messed it up, upside down.[sic]"

The transcripts reflect an effort to keep Mr. Salem as an intelligence asset who would not have to go public or testify.

What the article and no one else seems to cover is that whether or not the FBI messed up the substitution of a real bomb with a fake bomb, the fact is the FBI did nothing further to stop or at least warn people so they could have evacuated the building.

Earlier we provided details of a planned False Flag attempt called "Operation Northwoods" from 1962, but this wasn't the only attempted False Flag plan not to have been put into action. In July 2008, Pulitzer Prize winning journalist, Seymour Hersch in speaking at a journalism conference and writing for 'The New Yorker' on July 7, 2008 reveals how Vice President Cheney held meetings to discuss ways to provoke war with Iran.

Hersch stated:

> "There was a dozen ideas proffered about how to trigger a war. The one that interested me the most was why don't we build—we in our shipyard—build four or five boats that look like Iranian PT boats. Put Navy seals on them with a lot of arms. And next time one of our boats goes to the Straits of Hormuz, start a shoot-up. Might cost some lives."

Fortunately, just like Operations Northwoods, this plan was also rejected, but it goes to prove that the use of *False Flags* continue to be an option that our government considers, even if it results in U.S. casualties and, as we've seen, the deaths of millions of people.

Lastly, looking at two recent mass shootings in the U.S. that have led many to call for gun confiscation and restrictions and changes to the Second Amendment, we find numerous reasons to believe that these were staged and deliberate events to create a reaction of hate towards gun owners so that they can come in with the solution and attempt to disarm the people.

Both the "Batman" shooting in Aurora, CO on July 20th 2012 and the Sandy Hook Elementary School shooting in Newtown, CT on December 14th 2012 had so much in common it has to raise questions that I doubt will ever be answered officially. Here's just a few items that need closer inspection.

References to both 'Aurora' and 'Sandy Hook' can be seen in the Batman Movie "Dark Night Rising". A large neon "Aurora" sign is shown atop a building while Sandy Hook is the only legible name on a map that one of the characters points to.

Both shooters were prescribed with psychotropic drugs—although this is true of virtually all mass shootings.

Both had eye witness accounts from the shootings speaking of other shooters being very quickly shut down. In the Aurora shooting it was reported that just before the shooting started a man was called on his cell phone, he went to an exit door and opened it to allow the shooter to come in. Other witnesses spoke of smoke bombs going off at the opposite side of the theater. In the Sandy Hook shooting, eye witness reports of two and possibly three other shooters were heard. In one report a boy talks of a man being held on the ground and hand cuffed. Another report shows TV footage of a man being chased by police into the woods and another report taken from police radio talks of two men with guns coming towards them. The witness to the man that was chased in the woods said that he saw him later sitting in the front of a police car. Why would the police put a suspect in the front seat? Yet in both cases these reports are silenced.

There are several other oddities on each event.

James Holmes, the CO shooter was a student of neuroscience studying mind control. This ties in with an inmate report of James Holmes stating that "he was programmed to kill by an evil therapist".

In the Sandy Hook shooting it was first reported that two hand guns, a Glock and a Sig Sauer were found at the scene, but later the story is changed to an Assault Rifle using .223. Later still, NBC News reports that four handguns were used and that a rifle was found in Lanza's car, but it was not used. Given that some children were shot as many as eleven times this would require multiple magazines for each gun and to be on target so many times requires a lot of skill and training—do you smell anything rotten here?

The CT Police stated that anyone spreading false rumors of the shooting would be prosecuted—the only truth of the shooting was to come from them.

Not only did the usual gun control crowd use this as an excuse to come up with new gun control legislation but also the Chinese government calls for Americans to be disarmed and of course as reported on in the 'New American' January 24 2013:

"Communists Cheer on Obama's Gun Grab"

And most bizarre, a man supposed to be the father of one of the murdered children is captured on video just seconds before he goes on live television laughing and smiling and then suddenly after deep breathing talks of the pain he is suffering. I'm not saying for sure that this is fake, just seems bizarre to me.

Although some will still not admit it, we all *know* JFK was not simply shot by Lee Harvey Oswald so why do the majority go on believing what the experts on television are telling us?

Just as Zbigniew Brzezinski implied in his book Between Two Ages—we will soon not be able to have our own thoughts but just repeat what experts have told us on the news the night before.

And even on those rare occasions that a major event is not engineered you can guarantee that those 'bloodlines' we have been discussing will certainly not let it go to waste.

> "You never want a serious crisis to go to waste. And what I mean by that is an opportunity to do things you think you could not do before." Rahm Emanual, White House Chief of Staf, Video interview for the Wall Street Journal, 2008

There is one more False Flag event that needs to be explored . . .

CHAPTER 7

September 11th 2001

In September 2000 a 'think tank' *called The Project for the New American Century* issued a report titled 'Rebuilding America's Defenses'. In Section V of the report, titled 'Creating Tomorrow's Dominant Force' it states:

> "Further, the process of transformation, even if it brings revolutionary change, is likely to be a long one, absent some catastrophic and catalyzing event—like a new Pearl Harbor."

One year later they got their supercharged catalyzing event—9/11

On August 2 2008 both CNN and the Washington Post ran headlines that stated that 6 out of 10 on the 9/11 Commission distrusted the information they were being given by people within the Pentagon. Combine that with Senator Max Cleland's statement shown above, the question has to asked—if they don't believe what they were told then why should you?

Once again I ask you to put your 'Columbo' raincoat on, try your best to remove the obvious emotions that surround this subject and look logically at the evidence being presented.

Exhibit A—World Trade Center 7

World Trade Center (WTC) 7 was a forty seven story steel frame building that collapsed at near freefall speed into its own footprint through what was or logically should have been the path of greatest resistance at around 5:20pm, some twenty minutes *after* the BBC and CNN reported that it had collapsed. Given that such a steel frame building has never collapsed in the history of the world how is it possible they could predict this?

WTC 7 was not hit by a plane. It had a few small fires on three of the floors and yet we're told that this caused its total collapse. The only way a building of this size could collapse at near freefall speed is if all the supporting columns are cut simultaneously. This would not be possible without the use of controlled demolition. See for yourself by watching the video evidence.

Internet search term: **WTC 7 collapse**

Other than a brief footnote in the 9/11 Commission Report, WTC 7 was not mentioned.

Larry Silverstein, the owner of the WTC complex (we'll detail this later) stated on a PBS interview that:

> "I remember getting a call from the, er, fire department commander, telling me that they were not sure they were gonna be able to contain the fire, and I said, 'We've had such terrible loss of life, maybe the smartest thing to do is pull it.' And they made that decision to pull and we watched the building collapse."

In the construction and demolition industry, for which Silverstein is very familiar, the term 'pull it' is normally used when deliberately demolishing a building.

Video prior to the demolition of WTC 7 emerged that showed police telling people to get back because the building is about to come down. In one video you can even hear a countdown to its demolition.

Internet search term: **first responders heard WTC 7 demolition countdown**

Barry Jennings who was Deputy Director of Emergency Services went on record to speak about bombs exploding inside the building and below them as they were trying to exit via the stairwell between the 6th and 8th floors. This was even prior to the twin towers collapsing. Barry Jennings reportedly died on August 19 2008 at the age of fifty three and just two days before NIST released their final report on WTC 7.

With our raincoats on and cigar in hand we must now scratch our heads and ponder the question of why was WTC 7 demolished?

In addition to the normal financial institutions, WTC 7 was also home to the IRS Regional Council, U.S. Secret Service, C.I.A, Securities and Exchange Commission (SEC), Department of Defense and the Mayor's Office of Emergency Management (where Barry Jennings worked).

With such an interesting group of tenants and the presumably priceless amounts of data each of these must have held in this building, you have to wonder why it was left to the landlord, Larry Silverstein, to decide to 'pull it'—surely wouldn't these government agencies do their best to keep this building intact? Or perhaps we are on to something.

It was reported that the FBI, DOD and IRS had huge amounts of evidence in several corporate tax fraud cases, including that of Enron.

In fact Reuters and the L.A. Times published reports stating that the SEC had lost three thousand to four thousand active case files that would result in many cases being dropped and put others is serious jeopardy.

> . . . "Ongoing investigations at the New York SEC will be dramatically affected because so much of their work is paper-intensive," said Max Berger of New York's Bernstein Litowitz Berger & Grossmann. "This is a disaster for these cases."

Citigroup also stated that evidence, including back up date of emails pertaining to the Worldcom scandal were all destroyed.

Here's another interesting fact that might raise a few eyebrows. George W. Bush's brother, Marvin Bush, and his cousin, Wirt Walker III, were both principles in the company Stratesec, formerly named Securacom, that was in charge of security for the World Trade Center complex, with Wirt Walker being the CEO from 1999 until January 2002. Additionally, the COO of Stratesec was Barry McDaniel who came from a subsidiary of The Carlyle Group—we'll find other interesting links to The Carlyle Group later.

Another excellent source for anyone wanting to further research WTC 7 is Architects and Engineers for 9/11 Truth (www.ae911truth.org).

Exhibit B—The Pentagon

The official 9/11 Commission Report tells us that:

> "At 9:37, the west wall of the Pentagon was hit by hijacked American Airlines Flight 77, a Boeing 757. The crash caused immediate and catastrophic damage. All 64 people aboard the airliner were killed, as were 125 people inside the Pentagon (70 civilians and 55 military service members)"

Two days after 9/11 the Secretary of Defense, Donald Rumsfield, in an interview with Good Morning America is quoted as saying:

> "Yeah. And then came in about—between about the first and second floor over here. And it went in through three rings. I'm told the nose is—is still in there, very close to the inner courtyard, about one ring away."

According to Boeing, the wingspan of a 757 is 124ft 10inches, the exterior body width is 12ft 4 inches and the tail height is 44ft 6 inches.

On September 14 2001 the National Post in Canada printed a nine inch by 6 inch photograph of the Pentagon before the roof collapsed. It shows a hole at ground level with an approximate diameter of 16ft and with a car burning close by. If a Boeing 757 with its 124ft wingspan and 44ft tail did hit the Pentagon, what happened to the wings and tail section?

Major General U.S. Army, Commanding General of U.S. Army Intelligence and Security Command, Albert Stubblebine said:

> "I look at the hole in the Pentagon and I look at the size of an airplane that was supposed to have hit the Pentagon. And I said, 'The plane does not fit in that hole'. So what did hit the Pentagon?"

The early reports from the media specifically Jamie McIntyre of CNN reported that:

> "from my close up inspection there's no evidence of a plane having crashed anywhere near the Pentagon . . . there are no large tail sections, wing sections, a fuselage, anything like that around which would indicate that the entire plane crashed into the side of the Pentagon"

This video can be seen on my website:

www.thenewalexandrialibrary.com/pentagon.html

Aerial pictures of the Pentagon showed what appears to be exit holes, or at least that is what the official story tells us. On the third ring of the Pentagon and if Donald Rumsfeld was correct in his statement that the nose of the plane was still inside, close to the inner ring, how is it possible that a plane could impact the outer ring and then completely bypass the fourth ring to magically re-enter the third ring so that it could exit once more? Even David Copperfield would have difficulty pulling that off.

Norman Mineta, who at the time was Secretary of Transportation, testified on video the following to the 9/11 Commission:

> "During the time that the airplane was coming into the Pentagon, there was a young man who would come in and say to the Vice President . . . the plane is 50 miles out . . . the plane is 30 miles out . . . . and when it got down to the plane is 10 miles out, the young man also said to the vice president "do the orders still stand?" And the Vice President turned and whipped his neck around and said "Of course the orders still stand, have you heard anything to the contrary!?"

Why did the 9/11 Commission not include this or any reference to this statement in their final report?

There are many other anomalies that should at least raise more questions:

Why did the FBI confiscate eighty security tapes from businesses who were located close to where the plane was alleged to have crashed, but could only provide five small frames of an explosion, but nothing obvious to show a plane hitting the west wall?

Is it just a coincidence that the section of the Pentagon that was hit was the only section that had just been renovated and included a sprinkler system (not installed anywhere else) and was built with a web of steel columns that could withstand a bomb blast?

How is it possible for an untrained pilot to have completed what 'Pilots for 9/11 Truth' show to be an almost impossible maneuver?

Why was there no investigation into reports of a mysterious unmarked white plane seen flying over the Pentagon at around the same time.

Exhibit C—The Twin Towers

The building of the World Trade Center complex started in 1966. In a 1993 interview with John Skilling, the head structural engineer for the World Trade Center, he stated the Twin Towers were built to withstand a direct impact from a Boeing 707 or a Douglas DC-8 (Boeing 707 is only slightly smaller than a 767) by using a matrix of fifty nine steel columns per side and a steel and concrete core of forty seven columns that ran from bedrock to the top. Each tower had 110 floors. Skilling referred to how aircraft-impact analysis, involving impact of a Boeing 707 at 600 miles per hour (970 km/h) was used in the design. In recalling his analysis, he remarked:

> "Our analysis indicated the biggest problem would be the fact that all the fuel (from the airplane) would dump into the building. There would be a horrendous fire. A lot of people would be killed," he said. "The building structure would still be there."

American Airlines flight 11 crashed into floors 93 to 99 of the North Tower at 8:46 am. United Airlines Flight 175 crashed into the South Tower 17 minutes later at 9:03 am between floor 77 and 85.

The South Tower collapses at 9:59am and the North Tower collapses in identical fashion at 10:28am. The observed time for the total collapse of the South Tower was 10 seconds, this is confirmed in the 9/11 Commission Report. This means that the towers collapsed at near freefall speed and showing no resistance at all.

The National Institute of Standards and Technology (NIST) said they found that sagging floors pulled inward on the perimeter columns:

> "This led to the inward bowing of the perimeter columns and failure of the south face of WTC 1 and the east face of WTC 2, initiating the collapse of each of the towers."

Their theory would have us believe that as one floor gave way it would cause the floor below to collapse and so on for seventy plus floors. If this was true and the sagging floors simply piled up on each other how is it possible that the forty seven core columns were not left standing?

If the floors simply collapsed, how it is possible that bone fragments are found a decade later on buildings hundreds of feet away and how can massive steel beams be propelled like bullets into other buildings?

Here's a few more important items that raises serious questions.

Several live television reports including CNN and ABC News provide evidence of bombs exploding inside the buildings. In some of the videos the actual explosions can be heard. Other videos show fireman talking of bombs inside the buildings.

William Rodriguez, a janitor at the Twin Towers testified to the 9/11 Commission of bombs exploding in the basement. The 9/11 Commission Report does not provide any mention of bombs inside the buildings.

The official story detailed in the 9/11 Commission Report tells us that some of the hijackers were identified because their passports were found in the rubble of the WTC towers. Specifically, the passport of Satam al Suqami, who was alleged to be on AA Flight 11, was reportedly found at the base of the WTC. How is it possible that a paper passport, presumably in the jacket pocket of a hijacker, inside flight 11 was able to survive the impact of the plane crashing into the North Tower and the massive fireball that followed only to be found virtually unscathed when we're also told that everyone on that plane would have vaporized?

Physics Professor Steven Jones Ph.D. published a peer reviewed paper in 'The Open Physics Chemical Journal' in 2009 titled "Active Thermitic Material Discovered in Dust from the 9/11 World Trade Center Catastrophe" which details that after examining dust from the WTC collapse he discovered definite traces of nano-thermite, a material normally used to slice through steel in controlled demolitions. Combine this with reports of rivers of molten steel found in the rubble the Twin Towers suggests that the only logical explanation indicates that the towers were brought down by advanced demolition techniques.

In a live ABC News interview Mayor Giuliani stated that he was warned that the Towers would collapse. He said:

> "I went down to the scene and we set up headquarters at 75 Barkley Street, which was right there with the Police Commissioner, the Fire Commissioner, the Head of Emergency Management and we were operating out of there when we were told that the World Trade Center was going to collapse. And it did collapse"

As with all crimes it's vital that we look at who benefited?

On February 15, 2001, the Port Authority announced that Vornado Trust Realty had won the lease for the World Trade Center, paying $3.25 billion for the ninety nine year lease. Vornado Realty outbid Larry Silverstein by $600 million, though Silverstein upped his offer to $3.22 billion. However, Vornado insisted on last minute changes to the deal, including a shorter thirty nine year lease which the Port Authority considered non negotiable. Vornado later withdrew and Silverstein's bid for the lease to the World Trade Center was accepted on April 26, 2001 and closed on July 24, 2001.

It should also be noted that Vornado Realty Trust, whose chief shareholder and co-chairman was Bernard Mendik, was Silverstein's former brother-in-law. They had reportedly fallen out big time after his divorce from Silverstein's sister. On May 28th, just a few weeks after

Silverstein and his partner Frank Lowy presented their final bid for the WTC, Vornado's Bernard Mendik died of cardiac arrest.

Larry Silverstein was due to be at work on September 11th at his offices on the 88th floor of the North Tower but he told reporters that his wife insisted that he attend a dermatologist appointment instead. His son Roger and daughter Lisa would regularly have breakfast in the Windows on the World Restaurant, more than 100 floors up in the North Tower, but none of them showed on 9/11. It is also reported that one his bodyguards has said privately, he had a phone call in his car telling him to stay away from the World Trade Center that morning. He then got on his car phone to tell his children. (Source: David Icke 'They Dare Not Speak its Name')

Silverstein knew the towers required some $200 million in renovations and improvements, most of which related to removal and replacement of building materials declared to be health hazards in the years since the towers were built. He also made sure that the insurance policy with a value of $7.1 Billion, it included covering acts of terrorism.

After the attacks on 9/11 Silverstein filed TWO insurance claims for the maximum amount of the policy, based on the two, in Silverstein's view, separate attacks.

As reported in The Washington Post, the insurance company, Swiss Re, had gone to court to argue that the 9/11 disaster was only one attack, not two and that therefore the insurance payout should be limited to $3.55 billion, still enough to rebuild the complex.

A settlement was reached in 2004, with insurers agreeing to pay out $4.55 billion.

So, in summary, Silverstein buys WTC 1 & 2 for $3.22 Billion, he and his children 'luckily' do not go to the North Tower in the morning, he avoids costly renovations and makes a tidy $1.33 BILLION in profit.

Another important piece of evidence that also was not mentioned in the 9/11 Commission Report is that of George W. Bush's statement made in two separate town hall meetings, one on December 4 2001 and the other on January 5 2002. In December he was asked:

> "how did you feel when you heard about the terrorist attack?"

> BUSH: Well, Jordan, you're not going to believe what state I was in when I heard about the terrorist attack. I was in Florida. And my chief of staff, Andy Card, actually I was in a classroom talking about a reading program that works. And I was sitting outside the classroom waiting to go in, and I saw an airplane hit the tower. The TV was obviously on, and I use to fly myself, and I said 'there's one terrible pilot' And I said 'it must have been a horrible accident'. But I was whisked off there, I didn't have much time to think about it, and I was sitting in the classroom and Andy Card, my chief who was sitting over here walked in and said 'a second plane has hit the tower. America's under attack."

How can this be possible, when video of the first plane crashing into the tower did not surface until after the second plane had crashed?

The Principal of Booker Elementary school, Gwendolyn Tose-Rigell, when asked about Bush seeing the first plane said "absolutely not', there was no television in the corridor or anywhere near the classroom." When interviewed by MSNC she told them "I actually heard the first plane had hit from the president," since she had been with Bush prior to entering the classroom, wouldn't she have seen it too. And if there had been a television in the hallway that was tuned into the news, wouldn't the natural reaction from people to such a terrible scene be to flock around and watch?

Gwendolyn Tose-Rigell died in December 2007. The Herald Tribune reported "It is unclear how Tose-Rigell died".

Without the 'Terrorist attacks', September 11th was to be a big day for several government agencies. Once such agency was FEMA. Was it a coincidence that FEMA arrived in New York City the night before 9/11 for bio terror drill? FEMA spokesman told Dan Rather of CBS News that "we arrived on late Monday night and went into action on Tuesday."

Was it also a coincidence that NORAD was running multiple drills on 9/11 that included hijacked planes and thus caused so much confusion that hijacked planes were allowed to fly hundreds of miles without being intercepted? In a comment made by air traffic control personnel which was featured in a July 2004 BBC television report, the controller is told that a hijacked airliner is heading for New York and responds by saying,

"is this real world or an exercise?"

Was it a coincidence that on June 1 2001 the Chairman of the Joint Chief of Staff issued an instruction titled "Aircraft Piracy (Hijacking) and Destruction of Derelict Airborne Object" in which it changes it policy so that the Secretary of Defense must approve any intervention.

Was it a coincidence that John O'Neil died in 9/11? John O'Neil was heading up the hunt for Bin Laden at the F.B.I., but was constantly frustrated at what he felt was obstruction. He started his new job as head of security at WTC on 9/10.

Was it a coincidence that the week before 9/11 the volume of 'Put Options' (bets that a stock price would go down) was extraordinarily high.

Was it a coincidence that Donald Rumsfeld on 9/10 announced that the Pentagon had 'lost' $2.3 Trillion? After 9/11 that was all got forgotten.

Was it a coincidence that the Carlyle Group including George H.W. Bush and Shafig Bin Laden, brother to Osama, were meeting in a Washington hotel on 9/11 and that the Bin Laden plane was the only plane that was allowed to fly out of the U.S. once all other flights had been grounded. It should also be noted that the late brother of Osama, Salem bin Laden was a major investor in George W. Bush's first oil company, Arbusto Oil.

What are we to make of the five 'Israeli art students' who were seen recording the planes and celebrating as they crashed into the towers. The *five men were detained and questioned by the FBI who reported that bomb sniffing dogs reacted to clothing and residue found in the van they were using.* And yet they are released without charge and of course no mention in the 9/11 Commission Report.

And finally, what should we make of reports from Newsweek, L.A. Times, NY Times and Washington Post that six of the hijackers were being trained at Pensacola Naval Air Force base? Newsweek's article titled "Alleged Hijackers May Have Trained at U.S. Bases" details how five of the alleged hijackers were trained at U.S. military bases and that:

> "Three of the alleged hijackers listed their address on drivers licenses and car registrations as the Naval Air Station in Pensacola, Fla.-known as the 'Cradle of U.S. Navy Aviation,' according to a high-ranking U.S. Navy source"

Although we may never know exactly what happened and how, the evidence is clear—**9/11 *was* an *Inside job!***

And what of the supposed mastermind of 9/11, Osama bin Laden, the same Osama bin Laden whose CIA name was Tim Osman, the same Osama bin Laden who under the direction of the CIA and Zbigniew Brzezinski set up Al Qaeda to help the Mujahideen fight against the Soviets in Afghanistan during the 80's? Did it really take the most powerful country in the world ten years to capture and kill him or did he die in 2001 of Marfans Syndrome as was reported in several international newspapers and was confirmed by Dr. Steve Pieczenik M.D. Ph.D who served as a Deputy Assistant Secretary of State and/or Senior Policy Planner under Secretaries Henry Kissinger, Cyrus Vance, George Schultz and James Baker?

Even if we are to believe he survived that long, the inconsistency and pure fantasy of the stories and explanations of what was supposed to have happened are way beyond belief if they are looked at with an unbiased mind. First we are told that Osama was armed and shooting at the SEALs, then we are told he wasn't armed but was using his wife as a shield. Then we are told that his body was buried at sea within 24 hours in accordance with Muslim law—total B.S.

The compound in Abbottobad, Pakistan is 1,000 miles from the Arabian Sea where they are supposed to have dumped his body. To believe that the compound can be fully secured and that complete and proper identification with collection of supporting evidence could be accomplished, and the logistics to take his body 1,000 miles to a waiting ship to then drop his body in the sea—all within 24 hours? It should not be forgotten that a U.S. Black Hawk helicopter crashed during the raid on the compound and although the official story denies that any of the 23 SEALs were killed there had to be some injuries that needed to be taken care of.

You'd also have to believe that Osama must have had time to put a curse on the SEAL team that got him, since in addition to the crashed helicopter on the day of the supposed raid, another helicopter crashes this time killing 30 Americans and according to Fox News:

> "insurgents shot down a U.S. military helicopter during fighting is eastern Afghanistan, killing 30 Americans, most of them belonging to the same elite unit as the Navy SEALs who killed former Al Qaeda leader Usama Bin Laden.[sic]"

And on December 20 2012 reports surface that "US Navy SEAL commander, who killed Osama Bin Laden, commits 'apparent suicide' in Afghanistan.

Not many left to corroborate the official story—how convenient.

And then of course newspaper headlines like that from the Daily Mail reports:

'Revealed: Military emails show that NO U.S. sailors witnessed Osama Bin Laden's secret burial at sea"

Why did 9/11 happen? Apart from going to war in Afghanistan and then Iraq (although as Bush said, 'Iraq had nothing to do with 9/11') and setting up permanent military bases in the Middle East and awarding huge *no bid* contracts to *friends* of our leaders, one of the main reason was to pass the Patriot Act.

As George H.W. Bush said in a speech given September 11th 1991:

> "What is at stake is more than one small country. It's a big idea, a new world order."

From the Patriot Act we have given up many of our freedoms and it has become the platform for hundreds of Executive Orders and other laws such as the National Defense Authorization Act (NDAA) that will soon be used to enforce Martial Law with even more authoritarian rule that Hitler or Stalin had over their citizens. Without 9/11 none of this legislation could have passed.

Are you still wondering why Bush told the United Nations:

"Let us never tolerate outrageous conspiracy theories concerning the

attacks of September the 11"?

"The Justice Department has reported that a second explosive device has been found in the Oklahoma Federal Building. I'd like to tell you in addition to that, two different explosive devices were found in addition to what went off, a total of three. The first bomb that was in Federal Building did go off, the second was found and diffused, the third they are working on now; both the first and the second were larger than the first."—KFDR CHANNEL 5 NEWS

CHAPTER 8

Lies, Lies, Lies

In 1994, the Clinton Administration tried and failed to push through an Antiterrorist and Effective Death Penalty Bill. This was a major problem for the New World Order.

In 1995, following the bombing of the Alfred P. Murrah building in Oklahoma City, the reaction from the public was overwhelming.

In 1996 a solution to the problem is signed into law, The Anti terrorism and Death Penalty Act of 1996 and HABEAS CORPUS Reform.

Just as we've reviewed with 9/11, the official story of the Oklahoma City bombing is also full of holes.

If this was the work of Timothy McVeigh using only a truck bomb, why did we hear so many reports of a second and then a third bomb being found *inside* the building. How was McVeigh supposed to have got such huge military grade bombs into a government secured building?

The ATF were already on the scene in bomb squad gear—before the bombing. Did they know or get a tip off? And if so why didn't they warn everyone else?

Columns were knocked out that were further away from the blast than weaker columns that were closer to the blast that remained.

Seismographs indicated multiple blasts.

The collapsed columns and header beams fell straight down. A blast from the street would have sent them flying away from the blast. Only by using contact explosives in the columns would cause them to fall straight down.

Witnesses admitted they were pressured by the FBI to implicate McVeigh.

A member of the OKC Fire Department stated that he was called about a week before the bombing and told to be in a state of extra "readiness" because of a bomb threat to the federal building.

Police Sergeant Terrance Yeakey was one of the first on the scene and he quickly set about rescuing eight people from the rubble. He was about to receive the Medal of Valor when he committed 'Suicide'. How was Yeakey supposed to have killed himself? According to his death certificate (which can be found at: www.thenewalexandrialibrary.com/terryyeakey.html) he slashed himself eleven times on both forearms before cutting his own throat twice near the jugular vein. Then, apparently seeking a more private place to die, he crawled another mile of rough terrain away from his car and climbed a barbed wire fence, before shooting himself in the head with a small caliber revolver. What appeared to be rope burns on his neck, handcuff bruises to his wrists, and muddy grass imbedded in his slash wounds strongly indicated that he had some help in traversing this final distance.

The bullets entrance wound was in the right temple, above the eye. It went through the policeman's head and exited in the area of the left cheek, near the bottom of the ear lobe line. The trajectory was from a 40-45 degree angle above his head. There were no powder burns. No weapon was ever reported as found at the scene, but independent investigators speculated that had Yeakey shot himself with standard police issue—a Glock 9mm or a .357 Magnum, his head would have been far more destroyed than it apparently was.

In London 2005 British Prime Minister Tony Blair was in big trouble. He had just been sent a very clear message from the British nation; via the May 2005 General Election, in which he was almost voted out of power; the British people did not want British troops fighting in George Bush's War of Terror in the Middle-East. This was a problem. So, to be able to keep the British troops fighting in the Middle-East, Tony Blair desperately needed something to happen, something to create a reaction that would change the nation's mind.

July 7 2005, three bombs exploded in the London Underground and one bomb exploded on a London bus at Tavistock Square killing over 50 and wounding many more. *Home grown Islamist terrorist* were blamed for the bombings and Britain's participation in the war continued. But just as we've seen in 9/11 there were also *terror drills* being run on 7/7

Here's the transcript on an amazing interview with Peter Power of Visor Consultants and the BBC:

> PETER POWER: At half past nine this morning we were actually running an exercise for a company of over a thousand people in London based on simultaneous bombs going off precisely at the railway stations where it happened this morning, so I still have the hairs on the back of my neck standing up right now.

HOST: To get this quite straight, you were running an exercise to see how you would cope with this and it happened while you were running the exercise?

POWER: Precisely, and it was about half past nine this morning, we planned this for a company and for obvious reasons I don't want to reveal their name but they're listening and they'll know it. And we had a room full of crisis managers for the first time they'd met and so within five minutes we made a pretty rapid decision that this is the real one and so we went through the correct drills of activating crisis management procedures to jump from slow time to quick time thinking and so on.

Internet Search Term: **PETER POWER LONDON BOMBING: video**

Please think about that unbelievable set of coincidences for a few seconds, to let the implications of it sink in. Then, please ask yourself: what are the odds against all of that happening by chance? The only conclusion that can be made is that it was not a coincidence.

And again, just like 9/11 and OKC bombing there were many other anomalies with this event that I shall not go into in this book, but suggest that the keen researcher watch the film documentary "7/7 Ripple Effect".

Previously we saw how the mass shootings in Aurora, Colorado and Sandy Hook Elementary school, CT were *embedded* into the Batman movie "Dark Night Rising", so before we move on let's take a quick look at a few other 'coincidences' involving 9/11 and 7/7 that are too strong to ignore:

In 1997 the popular cartoon TV show aired an episode that had the Simpsons travel to New York City and we see Maggie Simpson holding a magazine that had the number 9 right next to the silhouetted image of the Twin Towers which appears as the number eleven. For copyright reasons it cannot be shown in this book, but just use the internet search term: **SIMPSONS 9/11: IMAGES** and see for yourself the amazing 'coincidence'.

In the film "The Matrix" the main characters passport, Nero, shows an expiry date of September 11 2001.

In the 1996 film "Independence Day" the camera provides a close up of a countdown clock that shows the time 9:11.

A card game called Illuminati was introduced in 1995 with one of the cards depicting two identical towers with a huge explosion in one of them—an obvious scene from 9/11. Another card depicts the Pentagon in flames.

Internet Search Term: **Illuminati Card Game twin towers**

The spin off of the popular TV series 'X Files' titled "The Lone Gunman" ran their pilot episode in June 2001. In this episode a plane is taken over by remote control and its target it the World Trade Center towers.

The bomb that exploded in London on 7/7 carried an advertisement for a London play. The sign read "Outright Terror, Bold and Brilliant".

Internet Search term: **LONDON BOMBING BOLD AND BRILLIANT: Images**

In 1991, about four years before the Oklahoma City Bombing, Martin Keating, the brother of Frank Keating (Governor of Oklahoma from 1995 to 2003) wrote a manuscript titled 'The Final Jihad'. It was not published until after the bombing, but the story was based on terrorist attack in Oklahoma City by a character called Tom McVey.

Are these just coincidences or are they subliminal messages—or perhaps, are they simply just for 'their' laughs?

CHAPTER 9

Journey to a Brave New World

Throughout this book I have included several quotes from Bertrand Russell's 1931 non-fictional book 'The Scientific Outlook'. Now it is time to look at another book written in 1931 and first published in 1932, this time the fictional writing of Aldous Huxley titled 'Brave New World'. Brave New World brings us a vision of the future where scientific and psychological techniques are used to genetically design humans to be passive and to perform certain tasks which are in support of a powerful ruling elite. The children that are raised as Alphas are the 'clever' ones and must wear grey clothing, whereas the Beta's, Delta's and Epsilons are progressively 'more stupid' and perform jobs suited to their genetically engineered capabilities. Humans are confined to cities and are restricted from traveling to certain areas without a very special permit. For those that live outside the confines of the controlling elites they are termed 'savages'. These savages live off the land and reproduce by giving birth the old fashioned way—there are very few savages.

Huxley does not explain how his vision for the future comes into being, but in his 1958 book "Brave New World Revisited" he compares the modern day world (of the late 50's) with his prophetic vision for the future described in 'Brave New World'. In this he also compares his vision with that of the book written by George Orwell (Eric Blair) in 1948 titled "1984". Another fictional book warning of what life would be like under a Totalitarian State. A world where everyone is monitored to ensure they comply with the rules of the tyrannical elites, a world where fear is used to fully control people and a world where freedom is a thing of the past.

Is the vision and warning of George Orwell's 1984 simply a long and painful stepping stone to Huxley's Brave New World?

Is there any evidence to suggest that humanity today is well down the path of a Brave New World. Is humanity being manipulated and engineered towards Huxley's vision such that only a small group of elite families or bloodlines will be the beneficiaries? Will we be required to go through a *1984* phase before it can emerge into *their* Brave New World?

One year after 1984 was published, Aldous Huxely wrote to George Orwell in which he said:

> "Within the next generation I believe that the world's rulers will discover that infant conditioning and narco-hypnosis are more efficient, as instruments of government, than clubs and prisons, and the lust for power can be just as completely satisfied by suggesting people into loving their servitude as by flogging and kicking them into obedience. In other words, I feel that the nightmare of *nineteen eighty-four* is destined to modulate into the nightmare of a world having more

resemblance to that which I imagined in *Brave New World*. Meanwhile, of course there may be a large scale biological and atomic war-in which case we shall have nightmares of other and scarcely imaginable kinds."

Aldous Huxley was born in 1894 and belonged to England's intellectual aristocracy. He had links to the Ava Alice Astor, an occultist and therefore could be considered as part of the ruling elite and ruling bloodlines, however, his book may also have been a warning to us. He concludes *Brave New World Revisited* by stating:

"Meanwhile there is still some freedom left in the world. Many young people, it is true, do not seem to value freedom. But some of us still believe that without freedom, human beings cannot become fully human and that freedom is therefore supremely valuable. Perhaps the forces that now menace freedom are too strong to be resisted for very long. It is still our duty to do whatever we can do to resist them."

Huxley was not the only one to conclude their writings in this way. Bertrand Russell concludes "The Scientific Outlook" with:

"So long as it is present, science, having delivered him from bondage to nature, can proceed to deliver him from bondage to the slavish part of himself. The dangers exist, but they are not inevitable, and hope for the future is at least as rational as fear."

Other authors writing in the 1930's were not so optimistic about humanities ability to change direction. In H.G. Wells' book first published in 1935 titled 'The Open Conspiracy", Paul Tice introduces the book as follows:

"This is a guidebook on world control and management, a program that Wells believed should be orchestrated (and would be successful) through what he called the "Open

Conspiracy". This conspiracy is fully outlined in this work and is designed to be run by many separate organizations working together, as opposed to being just run by one group. Is this required reading for the world's most powerful people? Maybe it is. Or maybe it should be."

Wells himself writes:

"There is a clear hope that, later, directed breeding will come within this scope, but that goes beyond his present range of practical achievement, and we need not discuss it further here. Suffice it for us here that the world community of our desires, the organized world community conducting and ensuring its own progress, requires a deliberate collective control of population as a primary condition."

Wells concludes this book with:

"A time will come when men will sit with history before them or with some old newspaper before them and ask incredulously, 'Was there ever such a world?'"

He wrote this almost eighty years ago and unfortunately I believe we are already at that point and unless there's a significant awakening to 'their' agenda and a global revolution against it, humanity is on the precipice for which there may be no turning back.

We must break free of our programming and we must do all we can to help other wake up to these satanic worshipping bloodlines. To do this we must admit there's a problem and then face it. We must recognize that we are living in a *1984* world and we must say NO!

"You've got to fight for what you want, for all that you believe, it's right to fight for want you want to live the way we please. And as long as we have done our best and no one can do more and love and life and happiness are well worth fighting for."—Lyrics from 70's TV show "The Flashing Blade

---

CHAPTER 10

Welcome to 1984

Although at the time of writing this we still maintain a good amount of freedoms, certainly this book would never have been allowed to have been published in Orwell's *1984*, but the technology and infrastructure, mostly paid for by U.S. taxpayers is ready and available AND being used. The Executive Orders and the re-education camps are primed and prepared. Yes, you did read it correctly—re-education camps.

To support this claim I suggest you research the following official U.S. Army documents:

Army Regulation 210-35 Installations Civilian Inmate Labor Program, issued January 14 2005

FM 3-39.40 Interment and Resettlement Operations, February 2010

Appendix K—Audiovisual Team

"The audiovisual team uses organic equipment to produce and disseminate products to the I/R (Internment and resettlement) facility population. The team supports the facility PSYOP program by disseminating entertainment products, such as videos and music. This team gives the tactical PSYOP detachment the ability to influence detainee and DC behavior by providing or withholding something of value to the population. When directed, the team disseminates products that support other PSYOP task force programs (reeducation, reorientation, post hostility themes)".

To further prove the point that we are indeed at the door step of the Orwellian nightmare, let's take a look at a few news headlines.

The Guardian, September 11 2012—CCTV cameras being used in school changing rooms and toilets.

"Anti-surveillance campaigners find average of 24 cameras in each secondary school that responded to the survey."

Courthouse News Service, October 9 2012—Tasered for suffering a seizure, man says

"The complaint states: "In response to a 911 call seeking medical assistance because plaintiff Scott Sheeley was suffering a seizure, City of Austin Police Officers and Gold Cross Ambulance Service paramedics went to Sheeley's home on a 'Sick Cared For' assignment. Instead of providing medical care, police officers, with the assistance of ambulance paramedics, violently restrained Sheeley, depressing his ability to breathe, and repeatedly shocked him with a Taser gun."

The article continues to detail that paramedics administered drugs to Sheeley that further restricted his ability to breathe and therefore causing a cardiac arrest and the permanent brain damage that resulted.

Of course the article does not demand to know why a Taser was used who clearly was not a threat to anyone.

ABC News—Technology, Is your TV Watching you? Latest models raise concern.

"Samsung's 2012 top-of-the-line plasmas and LED HDTVs offer new features never before available within a television including a built-in, internally wired HD camera, twin microphones, face tracking and speech recognition. While these features give you unprecedented control over an HDTV, the devices themselves, more similar than ever to a personal computer, may allow hackers or even Samsung to see and hear you and your family, and collect extremely personal data."

The Daily Mail, March 16 2012—The CIA wants to spy on you through your TV: Agency director says it will 'transform' surveillance

"When people download a film from Netflix to a flatscreen, or turn on web radio, they could be alerting unwanted watchers to exactly what they are doing and where they are. Spies will no longer have to plant bugs in your home—the rise of 'connected' gadgets controlled by apps will mean that people 'bug' their own homes, says CIA director David Petraeus. The CIA claims it will be able to 'read' these devices via the internet—and perhaps even via radio waves from outside the home."

International Business Times, November 26 2012—Spy Mannequins Monitor Shoppers' Buying Habits

"Next time you go shopping it may not only be the overzealous sales assistant watching your every move—the shop floor mannequins may be checking you out too. Stylishly dressed dummies equipped with hidden cameras are coming to a store near you . . . Using facial recognition software, Almax said its mannequins, which cost £3200 each, can profile the age, race and gender of shoppers allowing retailers to develop more effective marketing strategies."

CBS News March 8 2012—Suit: Schools Spied on Students via Webcams

"A suburban Philadelphia school district used school-issued laptop webcams to spy on students at home, potentially catching them and their families in compromising situations, a family claims in a federal lawsuit. Lower Merion School District officials can activate the webcams without students' knowledge or permission, the suit said. Plaintiffs Michael and Holly Robbins suspect the cameras captured students and family members as they undressed and in other embarrassing situations, according to the suit."

Daily Express, July 23 2009—Sin bins for worst families

"THOUSANDS of the worst families in England are to be put in "sin bins" in a bid to change their bad behaviour, Ed Balls announced yesterday.

The Children's Secretary set out £400million plans to put 20,000 problem families under 24-hour CCTV super-vision in their own homes.

They will be monitored to ensure that children attend school, go to bed on time and eat proper meals.[sic]"

The Daily Mail, October 27 2011—Big Brother is watching: Fears over 'homeland security' streetlights that can record your conversations and track your movements

"Like something out of a sinister Orwellian vision of the future, streetlights with the ability to monitor conversations and announce government warnings are being installed on American streets.

As part of a federally-funded project, manufacturers Illuminating Concepts have begun installing the system, dubbed 'Intellistreets' in the town of Farmington Hills, Michigan.

According to the company's video presentation the capabilities of the devices include homeland security, public safety, traffic control, advertising and video surveillance features."

The article continues to detail how street lights contain a speaker system to broadcast emergency alerts, a video display and is also equipped with proximity sensors capable of recording both pedestrian and road traffic. These streetlights were deployed in Middlesborough, UK in 2006 to blast warnings at people who were indulging in anti-social behavior. Finally, the article reminds readers of an earlier article that revealed that talking trash bins are being installed in London and Liverpool which feature celebrity voices thanking people for not dropping litter.

MSNBC News, December 7 2010, Homeland Security taps new partner in terror fight: Wal-Mart, By month's end, 588 stores will participate in 'See Something, Say Something' campaign.

"At least 200 Wal-Mart stores will roll out security announcements within 24 hours, Wal-Mart spokesman Dan Fogleman said. By month's end, 588 stores in 27 states will be participating in the program. A short video featuring Napolitano will appear on TV screens at select checkout lanes, asking Wal-Mart shoppers to contact local law enforcement to report suspicious activity."

Daily Mail, June 5 2012—New surveillance cameras will use computer eyes to find 'pre crimes' by detecting suspicious behaviour and calling for guards

"A new generation of computerized 'Big Brother' cameras are able to spot if you are a terrorist or a criminal—before you even commit a crime.

The devices are installed in places like train stations or public buildings where they scan passers by to see if they are acting suspiciously.

Using a range of in-built parameters of what is 'normal' the cameras then send a text message to a human guard to issue an alert—or call them."

RT.COM, December 4 2012—'Everyone in US under virtual surveillance'—NSA whistleblower

"The FBI records the emails of nearly all US citizens, including members of congress, according to NSA whistleblower William Binney. In an interview with RT, he warned that the government can use this information against anyone."

Singulartiyhub.com February 5 2009 DESIGNER BABIES—LIKE IT OR NOT, HERE THEY COME

"The Fertility Institutes recently stunned the fertility community by being the first company to boldly offer couples the opportunity to screen their embryos not only for diseases and gender, but also for completely benign characteristics such as eye color, hair color, and complexion. The Fertility Institutes proudly claims this is just the tip of the iceberg, and plans to offer almost any conceivable customization as science makes them available . . . Like it or not, the era of designer babies is officially here and there is no going back."

This is just a sampling of Orwellian technologies that are available and being used today. The book by Mark Dice titled "Big Brother—The Orwellian Nightmare Come True" provides a lot more detail including the use of Radio Frequency Identification (RFID), GPS and Psychotronic weapons and is well worth reading.

The *Designer Babies* article is clearly more *Brave New World* than *1984*, but as can be seen they are already laying the groundwork.

In addition to the 'Big Brother' technologies and the re-education camps we've already looked at, it's worth reviewing two other elements taken directly from *1984*—the use of a "boogey man" to keep us in fear and the constant contradictions of who the enemy is.

In 1984 we had Emmanuel Goldstein as the face of terror. Show his face or report a threat by him and the citizens in 1984 would bow down to anything. For ten years since 9/11 our *Emmanuel Goldstein* was Osama Bin Laden.

In 1984 we would be at war with East Asia and then reports would come out stating that in fact East Asia is our friend and we're actually at war with West Asia. Today, our biggest terrorist threat comes from Al Qaeda, but now at the same time as we learnt in Libya and Syria Al Qaeda is our friend and hence why we are supplying them with thousands of anti aircraft missile and other supplies.

Most of the technologies being used are to assist in identifying problem people, people that do not go along with their agenda and who would likely revolt against them. Lord Bertrand Russell wrote throughout the 30's, 40's and 50's stating that they would use scientific techniques to control the minds of the masses. They would also use the sciences to identify those who might pose a threat to their agenda. One example is using Behavior Analysis tools such as the DISC Assessment that many corporation use to "help them identify communication styles" among other behaviors. What most people participating in these assessments do not know is where and how the data is stored and just who has access to it. The DISC assessment is based on understand four personality traits: Dominance, Inducement, Submission, and Compliance

Most of the DISC Assessment questions are seemingly innocent but let's just take a look at a few choices to which you either need to respond to with Most Likely and Least Likely:

Group 4—Stand up to opposition
Group 7—not afraid to fight
Group 12—Non Confrontational, giving in
Group 19—Will do as told, follows leaders
Group 23—Avoid any conflict

Anyone responding *Most Likely* to these questions will be marked.

And who marks them? And for what purpose?

In May of 2010, The Defense Advanced Research Projects Agency (DARPA) issued a Request For Information (RFI) titled:

DARPA—SN-10—46 SUSPECTED MALICIOUS INSIDER THREAT ELIMINATION (SMITE).

In this RFI DARPA states:

> "Many attacks are combinations of directly observable and inferred events. Topics of interest to this RFI include, but are not limited to, techniques to
>
> (a) derive information about the relationship between deductions, the likely intent of inferred actions, and suggestions about what evidence might mean and
>
> (b) dynamically forecast context-dependent behaviors—both malicious and non-malicious. Also of interest are on-line and off-line algorithms for feature extraction and detection in enormous graphs (as in billions of nodes) as well as hybrid engines where deduction and feature detection mutually inform one another."

Essentially, they are creating a huge Database from which analysis can identify possible inferred threats.

It should be remembered that the "E" in SMITE means Elimination.

DARPA does not go into any details as to what data would be used, but continually use the phrase "Inside threat detection".

What will you do the next time you are asked to complete a DISC Assessment? Just say NO!

"Posterity, you will never know how much it cost the present generation to preserve your freedom. I hope you will make good use of it. If you do not, I shall repent in heaven that ever I took half the pains to preserve it"—John Adams

"The answer to 1984 is 1776"—Alex Jones, Infowars.com

CHAPTER 11

Its Time To Make A Stand

It is not inevitable that 'they' will win. We do not have to take the journey to a *Brave New World* via *1984*. People are awakening and it's causing 'them' concern.

In a speech given in Poland towards the end of 2012, Zbigniew Brzezinski warned fellow elites that a worldwide resistance movement to external control is threatening to derail the move towards a New World Order.

Secretary of State Hilary Clinton in 2011 stated:

"We are in an information war and we are losing that war,"

Any psychologist or therapist will agree that in order to make a change you have to admit there's a problem. I hope that this book has provided the evidence to at least make you question what is really happening in this world.

Now you have this information what will you do? Will you make a stand?

Where would the United States be if people like Paul Revere and Samuel Adams decided to look the other way and do nothing?

I suggest that doing nothing is not a strategy that will favor you and your family, but that's exactly what 'they' are counting on. Making a stand and doing something may appear to be scary, but if we the people let this happen by acquiescing to 'their' plan, it will be a whole lot scarier.

I cannot say I know the exact details of what will happen and when, but there's a great deal of evidence for the following scenarios to be played out:

Global Financial Collapse—the total destruction of the U.S. Dollar, massive tax increases and 'Austerity measures'. The aim is to introduce their solution which will be a cashless society and one world currency.

Martial Law and the Second American Civil War—the stockpiling of weapons and ammo by the Department of Homeland Security and the coming gun confiscation is designed to push Americans to their limits and beyond. The NDAA, the Executive Orders, the FEMA Camps and the UN agreements to have troops on U.S. soil are in place and ready for the kick off.

Middle East war extending to World War III—there plan is to physically and mentally exhaust the people of the world so that "they" can provide the solution—a One World Government.

Communist Take Over—Russia and China were set up, encouraged and helped by the Western Ruling class (the New World Order) for one reason—Russian and Chinese troops will be used to complete the takeover of the United States. The *elites* have known for over a hundred years that taking down to U.S. would be their hardest task and collapsing the economy and constant war would not be enough. They need the people of America disarmed so that a Communist takeover would be quick. It is not beyond possibility that the billions of rounds of ammo being purchased will be used to re-supply communist troops.

Biological attack to achieve their required population levels—If war and famine does not meet their targets they will release deadly bio weapons. They may have already done this using nano technologies or binary bio weapons that can be triggered by a specific vector being added.

Shutdown of the Internet and power outages—this has been the central theme of many TV shows and movies as well as government plans such as the Cyber Security bills and Stuxnet, so I fully expect long periods of time with power and of course the internet.

Aliens—they do have plans to fool the world into believing that our planet is under attack. 'Project Blue Beam' is a NASA plan to use holographic technologies to fake a visitation and *external* threat.

Nuclear False Flag—as we have seen, television shows, movies and cartoons are used *predict* future engineered events. The TV show "Jericho" was not exactly subtle. It was based on how a community tried to survive America after the multiple simultaneous nuclear attacks on the U.S. At the end of the show we learn that it was government insiders that carried out the attack. Then we have Operation Blackjack—a comic strip style story that was published in the Telegraph which depicts multiple nuclear bombs exploding in the U.S. and London. Riots and Martial Law ensue and people are issued with a one world I.D. card and implanted RFID chip. The I.D. card shown in the story provides a long hexadecimal number which when put into a hex to decimal converter reads "This is not simply entertainment". At the end of this story we again discover the attacks were another *Inside job*. This is of particular concern when on march 26 2012 Bloomberg reports "Missing Nukes Fuel terror Concern as Obama Drawn to Seoul".

Get educated, get prepared and get active. We have a short period of time to make a difference.

As I stated in the introduction, this book only covers a small amount of what is really going on. I suggest in depth research on the following topics that I've either not covered in this book or have just provided a small taste:

Chemtrails—the deliberate release of gases and particles in our atmosphere.

Agenda 21—the United Nations Agenda for the 21st Century

FEMA Camps—REX 84, operation garden Plot, Civilian inmate labor program and Clergy Response Teams.

HAARP—High Frequency Active Aural Research Project used for Weather Manipulation, engineering earthquakes and mass mind control.

Barry Soetoro—the real name of the current U.S. President.

Humanity can survive, our children can have a future, but everyone must do their part. You must admit the problem and commit to making a difference and commit to making a stand. And you must start today, procrastination is not an option.

I am not suggesting that you stand in the center of town holding signs to alert the people (I've done that and unless you're in a large group it has minimal impact and high exposure), but you can keep it simple and reduce your exposure by gifting this book to close friends and family. Help others to wake up and always say NO! to their agenda.

NO to gun confiscation or regulations
NO to GMO foods
NO to Fluoridated Water
NO to big government
NO to forced vaccination
NO to full body scanners

Start asking the difficult questions when the next big event takes place.

And remember fear is the enemy, love is answer.

"Love is the answer, and you know that for sure"—John Lennon, Mind Games

BIBLIOGRAPHY

1. 9/11 Commission Report
2. Aldous Huxley, "Brave New World" (Harper Perennial)
3. Aldous Huxley, "Brave New World Revisited", (Harper Perennial) Letter to George Orwell
4. Zbigniew Brzezinski, "Between Two Age, America's Role in the Technetronic Era" (Viking Press, New York 1970 p11
5. Ibid, P 15
6. Bertrand Russell, "The Scientific Outlook" P 237
7. Ibid, P 194-195
8. Ibid. P 222
9. Ibid, P 258-259
10. Ibid, P 269
11. Bertrand Russell, "The Impact of Science on Society" (Routledge Taylor & Francis Group, 1952)P 116
12. Ibid, P 62
13. J.M. Roberts, "Europe 1880-1945" (second edition 1989) P 362-363
14. Club of Rome, "The First Global Revolution" P 75
15. Alberto Giubilini and Francesca Minerva, "After-Birth abortion: why should the baby live?", (BMJ Publishing March 2012)
16. Margaret Sanger, "Women and the New Race"(New York: Brentano's 1920) Chapter 5
17. Martin Meyer, "The Bankers, The Next Generation" (Truman Talley Books/Dutton 1997) P 41-42
18. Ibid, P42-43
19. G. Edward Griffin, "The Creature from Jekyll Island" (American Media, Fifth Edition 2010)
20. Ibid, P162

21. Ibid, P 224-227
22. Ibid, P 246-252
23. Ibid, P 3-23
24. Ibid, P 375
25. Max Hastings, "the Korean War" (Touchstone 1987) P 99-109
26. Ibid, p 128-146
27. Ibid, P 337
28. W. Cleon Skousen, "The Naked Communist" (Buccaneer Books, New York 1961) p 183
29. Ibid, P 101
30. Ibid, P 112
31. Ibid, P194
32. Ibid, P190-191
33. Ibid, P 259-262
34. W. Cleon Skousen, "The Naked Capitalist" P 78
35. Gary Allen with Larry Abraham, "None Dare Call it Conspiracy" (Concord Press 1972) P98-111
36. Ibid, P 102-103
37. David Icke, "The David Icke guide to the Global Conspiracy (and how to end it), (David Icke Books Ltd, 2007) P210-211
38. Ibid, P103
39. Ibid, P 212-213
40. Ibid, P116
41. David Icke, "Remember Who You Are", (David Icke Books Ltd, 2012) P 203-227
42. Ibid, P 392
43. Anthony C. Sutton, "Wall Street and the Bolshevik Revolution", (Veritas Publishing Company 1981) P 21-29
44. Ibid, P 39
45. Ibid, P158-159
46. Anthony C. Sutton, "Wall Street and the Rise of Hitler", (GSG & Associates 2002)
47. Ibid, P71
48. Ibid, P 93
49. David Irving, "Hitler's War" (Focal Point Publication, 2002) P 217

50. Edwin Black, "IBM and the Holocaust", (three Rivers Press, New York 2001) Back Cover

51. John Koster, "Operation Snow", (Regnery Publishing 2012) Cover

52. Ibid, P 46

53. David Irving, "Churchill's War", (Avon Books, 1991) P584-585

54. Robert K Wilcox, "Target: Patton", (Regnery Publishing, 2008) P 284-289

55. J.R. Church, "Guardians of the Grail", (Prophecy Publications, 1989) Chapter 5

56. Fritz Springmeier, "Bloodlines of the Illuminati" (Pentracks Publications Third Edition, 2007) P369-408

57. Ibid, P32

58. John Holdren, Paul Ehrlich, Anne Ehrlich, "Ecoscience—Population, Resources, Environment" (1997) P 786

59. Edward Bernays, "Propaganda", (Ig Publishing, first published 1928) P 37

60. Jim Marrs, "The Rise of the Fourth Reich", (Harper, 2008) P 21-22

61. H. G. Wells, "The Open Conspiracy", (The Book Tree, 2006-Original Publication C.A. Watt & Co. Ltd. 1935) Introduction

62. Ibid, P47

63. Ibid, P 150

64. Rebuilding America's Defenses—A report of the Project for a new American century, September 2000 P 51

OTHER SOURCES:

1. Harvard Law School Library—Nuremberg Trials Project

2. The Truth About Aspartame, MSG and Excitotoxins, with Mike Adams

3. Mark Dice, "Big Brother—The Orwellian Nightmare Come True"

4. Joseph Borkin, "The Crime and Punishment of I.G. Farben", (The Free Press, 1978)

5. Daniel Estulin, "The True Story of The Bilderberg Group", (Trineday, 2007)
6. Carroll Quigley, "The Anglo-American Establishment", (GSG & Associates, 1981)
7. ALEX JONES, INFOWARS.COM
8. LOOSE CHANGE, DVD
9. Alex Jones, "Endgame—Blueprint for Global Enslavement" DVD
10. Alex Jones, "Fall of the Republic" DVD
11. Alex Jones, "The Obama Deception" DVD
12. Alex Jones, "Terrorstorm" DVD
13. Alex Jones, "Police State 4", DVD
14. Rick Wiles, Trunews.com
15. National Security Study Memorandum 200 (NSSM200), December 10, 1974
16. Unmanned Ground Systems Roadmap—Robotic Systems Joint Project Office, July 2011
17. Second Trimester Abortion: From Every Angle, December 1992
18. Army Regulation 210-35, Civilian Army Inmate Labor Program
19. US Army Interment and Resettlement Field Manual
20. Department of Army, FM 3-19.15 Civil Disturbance Operations
21. A Noble Lie: Oklahoma City 1995 (2011) DVD